Guide to Martin's Annual Criminal Code

THIRD EDITION

Lance Triskle

In association with Thomson Reuters Canada Limited, publisher of
Martin's Annual Criminal Code 2020, edited by Marie Henein. In memory
and acknowledgment of the contributions of the late Honourable
Mr. Justice Marc Rosenberg and the late Edward L. Greenspan.
Reproduced with permission, 2020.

emond ▪ Toronto, Canada ▪ 2020

Emond Montgomery Publications Limited
1 Eglinton Avenue E, Suite 600
Toronto ON   M4P 3A1
https://www.emond.ca/highered

Printed in Canada.

We acknowledge the financial support of the Government of Canada and the Government of Ontario.

Emond Montgomery Publications has no responsibility for the persistence or accuracy of URLs for external or third-party Internet websites referred to in this publication, and does not guarantee that any content on such websites is, or will remain, accurate or appropriate.

In association with Thomson Reuters Canada Limited, publisher of *Martin's Annual Criminal Code 2020*, edited by Marie Henein. In memory and acknowledgment of the contributions of the late Honourable Mr. Justice Marc Rosenberg and the late Edward L. Greenspan. Reproduced with permission, 2020.

Vice president, publishing: Anthony Rezek
Publisher: Lindsay Sutherland
Director, development and production: Kelly Dickson
Production supervisor: Anna Killen
Production editor: Natalie Berchem
Copy editor: Holly Dickinson
Typesetter: Amnet
Proofreader: Tara Tovell
Cover designer: Jordan Bloom
Printer: Marquis

Library and Archives Canada Cataloguing in Publication

Title: Guide to Martin's annual criminal code / Lance Triskle.

Other titles: Guide to (work): Martin's annual criminal code

Names: Triskle, Lance, author.

Description: Third edition

Identifiers: Canadiana 20200207067 | ISBN 9781772557411 (softcover)

Subjects: LCSH: Canada. Criminal Code. | LCSH: Criminal law—Canada—Textbooks. | LCGFT: Textbooks.

Classification: LCC KE8809 .T75 2020 | LCC KF9220.ZA2 T75 2020 kfmod | DDC 345.71—dc23

To Sara, Emma, Hannah, and family.

—LT

BRIEF CONTENTS

Contents vii

Preface xi

About the Author xiii

CHAPTER 1   Introduction to Martin's Annual Criminal Code 1

CHAPTER 2   Table of Contents and Page Numbering...................... 3

CHAPTER 3   The Criminal Code... 9

CHAPTER 4   Index 19

CHAPTER 5   Offence Grid 23

CHAPTER 6   Table of Cases 41

CHAPTER 7   Criminal Code Concordance 45

CHAPTER 8   Commentary: Cross-References, Synopsis, and
             Annotations.. 55

CHAPTER 9   Shaded Text.. 73

CHAPTER 10   Forms.. 77

CHAPTER 11   Appendix / Forms of Charges 83

CHAPTER 12   Conclusion 95

CONTENTS

Brief Contents   v

Preface   xi

About the Author   xiii

1   Introduction to Martin's Annual Criminal Code.   1

2   Table of Contents and Page Numbering.   3

3   The Criminal Code.   9

Organization   9
   Introduction   9
   Numbering System.   9
   Parts, Topic Categories, and Sections   12
Definitions   12

4   Index.   19

5   Offence Grid   23

Introduction.   23
Type of Offence   23
   Indictable Offences.   23
   Summary Conviction Offences   28
   Hybrid Offences   28
Maximum/Minimum Sentence.   31

Available Sentences 32
   Discharge. 32
   Other Available Sentences. 34
Other Court Orders 36

6   Table of Cases.   41

7   Criminal Code Concordance.   45

Amendments to the Code 45
Revision of a Statute 46
Researching Judicial Decisions 46
Historical Offences: "Cold Cases". 50
Legislative History. 52

8   Commentary: Cross-References, Synopsis, and Annotations   55

Introduction. 55
Cross-References 55
Synopsis 58
Annotations 60
   Stare Decisis 61
   Disagreement Among Courts 62
   Ratio Decidendi and Obiter Dicta 64
   Case Name or Style of Cause 64
   Legal Citations. 65
   Infra and Supra 68
   Impact of the Charter on Judgments 69

9   Shaded Text.   73

Introduction. 73
Amendments 73
Regulations 73
Editor's Note 75

10 Forms 77

Introduction.   77
Application of Forms.   77

11 Appendix / Forms of Charges 83

Introduction.   83
Information (Form 2).   83
Correctly Completing the Information (Form 2).   84
Elements of the Offence and Sentencing   84
Requirements for an Information (Form 2)   87
  Drafting (Section 581 of the Code)   87
  Drafting an Information   87
  Multiple Accused   89
  Multiple Charges   90
  Details Missing (Section 583 of the Code)   90
  Particulars (Section 587 of the Code)   90

12 Conclusion. 95

What Is Martin's Annual Criminal Code?

Martin's Annual Criminal Code is an integral text for community safety teachers, students, and professionals. It includes legislation and analysis of criminal law in Canada. However, how does a reader navigate Martin's?

Why Was the Guide Created?

The third edition of the *Guide to Martin's Annual Criminal Code* was written specifically for novice users of Martin's and assists readers in navigating the book. Through new and revised examples and exercises, readers will grasp the relevant data in Martin's. The Guide demonstrates all the features in the book, including the Offence Grid, *Criminal Code* Concordance, and Commentary. Readers will also learn to use forms and correctly complete an Information.

Examples

The Guide has examples relevant to community safety professionals. The examples illustrate how to locate specific aspects of Canadian law in Martin's and include extracts of pages from the book, providing a step-by-step process for readers to follow while using the features in Martin's. Readers may also choose to use a copy of Martin's and the Guide together while exploring the examples.

Exercises

The exercises in the Guide invite readers to apply the knowledge from the examples to reinforce their learning. Once readers feel comfortable with Martin's, they can progress to navigating other annotated texts.

ABOUT THE AUTHOR

Lance Triskle is a professor in the community safety programs at Georgian College. His education and experience include dispute resolution and law. He currently teaches Indigenous Justice: Advocacy and Community Development, Dispute Resolution, and Criminal Law. He has a Bachelor of Arts from the University of Western Ontario, a Bachelor of Laws from Queen's University, a Teaching and Training Adults Certificate from Georgian College, and a Master of Laws from Osgoode Hall Law School at York University. He enjoys running, reading, and travelling with his family.

CHAPTER 1

Introduction to Martin's Annual Criminal Code

Anyone can navigate *Martin's Annual Criminal Code* (Toronto: Carswell, 2019)! This guide is a systematic approach to mining all of the data contained in Martin's.

The more familiar you become with the guide, the more you will appreciate the information in Martin's.

Martin's helps you analyze procedural and substantive Canadian criminal law. Often your research will be complete after reviewing the information found in Martin's. The guide will help you learn how to find what you need quickly and easily and benefit from the breadth and depth of information within Martin's.

Martin's reproduces the *Criminal Code*, R.S.C. 1985, c. C-46, in full, with extensive commentary researched and written by experts in Canadian criminal law. The commentary has three parts: Cross-References, Synopsis, and Annotations. The Government of Canada publishes the Code online; however, Martin's adds the commentary to each section to provide a better understanding of the legislation.

Martin's also includes the *Canadian Charter of Rights and Freedoms*, Part I of the *Constitution Act, 1982*, being Schedule B to the *Canada Act 1982* (UK), c. 11, with commentary. Additionally, Martin's includes other selected federal statutes with commentary, specifically the *Canada Evidence Act*, R.S.C. 1985, c. C-5; the *Controlled Drugs and Substances Act*, S.C. 1996, c. 19; and the *Youth Criminal Justice Act*, S.C. 2002, c. 1. Together, the Charter and these statutes govern the practice of criminal law. Further legislation is available in a similar format in *Martin's Related Criminal Statutes* (Toronto: Carswell, 2019).

Martin's has other features, such as the Code Concordance and the Offence Grid, that provide valuable information. We will discuss these tools later.

Using this guide to learn how to navigate Martin's will assist you with reading other annotated statutes, such as *The Annotated Tremeear's Criminal Code* (Toronto: Carswell, 2019), *The Practitioner's Criminal Code* (Toronto: LexisNexis, 2020), and *The Annotated Ontario Highway Traffic Act* (Toronto: Carswell, 2019).

CHAPTER 2

Table of Contents and Page Numbering

The Table of Contents lists the legislation and other navigational aids in the order in which they appear in *Martin's Annual Criminal Code*. It also provides the page references for easy searching.

Most of Martin's—over 1,800 pages—is made up of the *Criminal Code.* Following the Code are the *Canada Evidence Act*, the *Canadian Charter of Rights and Freedoms*, and other selected federal statutes. There are also aids to navigating Martin's indicated by page numbers that include an abbreviation. For example, the first page of the Table of Contents is C/1, the first page of the Preface is P/1, and the first page of the Offence Grid is OG/1. The abbreviations are:

Table of Contents	C
Preface	P
Criminal Code Concordance	CON
Table of Cases	TC
Offence Grid	OG
Index	IN
Index to Forms for the Criminal Code	IF
Appendix/Forms of Charges	A

Once you learn the abbreviations, you will more efficiently navigate your way through Martin's. Page numbers are listed at the bottom of the page.

Example 2.1

During class, your professor discusses the offence of possession of a weapon for a dangerous purpose under section 88 of the Code. The professor asks, "What is a weapon?" When you turn to page 199 (reproduced below), you find section 88 of the Code followed (on page 200) by the heading "Meaning of 'weapon.'"

On page 200 of Martin's (reproduced below), there are court interpretations of the word "weapon" along with a discussion of court decisions that answer the question "What is a weapon?"

Example 2.2

Your professor then discusses how the Charter protects people from unreasonable search and seizure. The professor suggests that you look on page 1920 of Martin's (reproduced below). On page 1920, you will find section 8 of the Charter. Section 8 ensures that "everyone has the right to be secure against unreasonable search or seizure."

EXERCISES

2.1   What is on page TC/1?

_____

_____

_____

_____

2.2   What is on page C/1?

_____

_____

_____

_____

2.3   What is on the first page of the *Youth Criminal Justice Act*?

_____

_____

_____

_____

(*b*) **is guilty of an offence punishable on summary conviction. 1995, c. 39, s. 139.**

CR. CODE

CROSS-REFERENCES
"Firearm" is defined in s. 2. Where the prosecution elects to proceed by way of summary conviction then the trial of this offence is conducted by a summary conviction court pursuant to Part XXVII. The punishment for the offence is then as set out in s. 787 and the limitation period is set out in s. 786(2). In either case, release pending trial is determined by s. 515, although the accused is eligible for release by a peace officer under ss. 496, 497 or by the officer in charge under s. 498.
    A person found guilty of the offences in this section is liable to the discretionary prohibition order prescribed by s. 110, unless the accused was prohibited from possessing weapons or other regulated items at the time of the offence, in which case the mandatory prohibition order in s. 109 applies.
    Note mandatory forfeiture of weapons used in commission of an offence in s. 491.

SYNOPSIS
This section creates the offence of pointing a firearm at another person without lawful excuse. The offence is committed whether or not the firearm was loaded.

ANNOTATIONS
The offence created by this section is one of general intent for the purpose of the self-induced intoxication defence: *R. v. Kelly* (1984), 13 C.C.C. (3d) 203, 50 Nfld. & P.E.I.R. 106 (Nfld. Dist. Ct.).

EXAMPLE 2.1
INTERPRETATION
BY COURTS

Possession Offences

POSSESSION OF WEAPON FOR DANGEROUS PURPOSE / Punishment.

88. (1) Every person commits an offence who carries or possesses a weapon, an imitation of a weapon, a prohibited device or any ammunition or prohibited ammunition for a purpose dangerous to the public peace or for the purpose of committing an offence.

(2) Every person who commits an offence under subsection (1)
    (*a*) is guilty of an indictable offence and liable to imprisonment for a term not exceeding ten years; or
    (*b*) is guilty of an offence punishable on summary conviction. 1995, c. 39, s. 139.

CROSS-REFERENCES
"Weapon" is defined in s. 2. "Prohibited device", "ammunition" and "prohibited ammunition" are defined in s. 84(1). "Possession" is defined in s. 4(3). Section 117.13 allows for the admission into evidence of a certificate of an analyst who has examined the weapon, prohibited device, ammunition, prohibited ammunition, explosive substance, or any part or component of such a thing.
    An accused charged with this offence may elect the mode of trial pursuant to s. 536(2) where the Crown proceeds by way of indictment. Where the prosecution elects to proceed by way of summary conviction then the trial of this offence is conducted by a summary conviction court pursuant to Part XXVII. The punishment for the offence is then as set out in s. 787 and the limitation period is set out in s. 786(2). In either case, release pending trial is determined by s. 515, although the accused is eligible for release by a peace officer under ss. 496, 497 or by the officer in charge under s. 498.
    A person found guilty of the offences in this section is liable to the discretionary prohibition order prescribed by s. 110, unless the accused was prohibited from possessing weapons or other

(Continued on the next page.)

regulated items at the time of the offence, in which case the mandatory prohibition order in s. 109 applies.

Note mandatory forfeiture of weapons used in commission of an offence in s. 491.

SYNOPSIS

The crucial element in this offence is the purpose for which the accused has the weapon. Merely using the weapon in a way which is in fact dangerous will not make out the charge unless it is proven that this was the accused's purpose for possessing the weapon or other specified thing. All circumstances surrounding the possession of the weapon, or specified thing including its use, if any, will be considered to determine the accused's purpose.

ANNOTATIONS

Note: The following cases were decided under the predecessor to this section which while similarly worded applied only to weapons and imitations of weapons.

Elements of offence – The offence contrary to this section requires proof of possession and proof that the purpose of that possession was one dangerous to the public peace. There must, at some time, be a meeting of these two elements and generally the purpose will have been formed prior to the taking of possession and will continue as possession is taken. However, the elements of the offence must be distinguished from the evidentiary problems which can arise as demonstrated by cases such as *R. v. Proverbs, infra,* where the proof of the unlawful purpose is only through the actual use of the weapon. In this case, *R. v. Cassidy,* [1989] 2 S.C.R. 345, 50 C.C.C. (3d) 193, 71 C.R. (3d) 350 (7:0), the court held that it did not have to determine whether the accused could never be convicted if the actual use was the only evidence of the purpose since there was evidence adduced of formation of the unlawful purpose prior to use of the weapon.

The purpose for which the accused had possession of the weapon must be determined at an instant of time that precedes its use. The use of the weapon in a manner dangerous to the public peace does not constitute the offence although the formation of the unlawful purpose may be inferred from the circumstances in which the weapon was used. Thus, if the accused, in fear of harm to himself in his own home loaded, on the sudden, a weapon that he had not had for a purpose dangerous to the public peace and only intended to use it to defend himself in the event that his premises were broken into, unaware that it was the police seeking entry to execute a warrant, the offence was not made out: *R. v. Proverbs* (1983), 9 C.C.C. (3d) 249, 2 O.A.C. 98 (C.A.).

Relevance of self-defence – The subjective purpose, *i.e.,* self-defence, of a person carrying an offensive weapon is only a factor that should be considered in determining whether an offence has been committed. Therefore, notwithstanding the explanation given by the possessor of the weapon, the trial judge may still convict if the other circumstances in the evidence prove a purpose dangerous to the public peace: *R. v. Nelson* (1972), 8 C.C.C. (2d) 29, [1972] 3 O.R. 174 (C.A.) (4:1).

This section does not prohibit persons arming themselves for self-protection and, in the absence of other circumstances, the offence under this section is not committed if the accused carries for self-defence a weapon that is an appropriate instrument with which to repel, in a lawful manner, the type of attack reasonably apprehended and if the accused is competent to handle the weapon and likely to use it responsibly: *R. v. Sulland* (1982), 2 C.C.C. (3d) 68, 41 B.C.L.R. 167 (C.A.).

Meaning of "weapon" – A broken beer bottle was held to be a weapon so as to support a conviction under this section: *R. v. Allan* (1971), 4 C.C.C. (2d) 521, 4 N.B.R. (2d) 6 (Q.B.). As also was sulphuric acid where the accused intended to inflict injury, albeit to himself in a suicide attempt. The further element of the purpose dangerous to the public peace was established where the accused exposed others to danger, namely those whom he knew would attempt to frustrate his suicide: *R. v. Dugan* (1974), 21 C.C.C. (2d) 45 (Ont. Prov. Ct.). Similarly, *R. v. Pelly*, [1980] 1 W.W.R. 120 (Sask. Prov. Ct.).

Proof of offence – The possession by the accused of weapons in his own home does not preclude a finding of a purpose dangerous to the public peace: *R. v. Stavroff*, [1980] 1 S.C.R. 411, 101 D.L.R. (3d) 193, 48 C.C.C. (2d) 353 (7:0).

CARRYING WEAPON WHILE ATTENDING PUBLIC MEETING / Punishment.

89. (1) Every person commits an offence who, without lawful excuse, carries a weapon, a prohibited device or any ammunition or prohibited ammunition while the person is attending or is on the way to attend a public meeting.

(2) Every person who commits an offence under subsection (1) is guilty of an offence punishable on summary conviction. 1995, c. 39, s. 139.

CROSS-REFERENCES

"Weapon" is defined in s. 2. "Prohibited device", "ammunition" and "prohibited ammunition" are defined in s. 84(1).

The trial of this offence is conducted by a summary conviction court pursuant to Part XXVII. The punishment for the offence is set out in s. 787 and the limitation period is set out in s. 786(2). Release pending trial is determined by s. 515, although the accused is eligible for release by a peace officer under ss. 496, 497 or by the officer in charge under s. 498.

Under s. 117.11, the onus is on the accused to prove that he or she is the holder of a licence, authorization or registration certificate. Section 117.12 provides for admission into evidence of copies of such documents and the evidentiary value of the original and copies. Section 117.13 allows for the admission into evidence of a certificate of an analyst who has examined the weapon, prohibited device, ammunition, prohibited ammunition, explosive substance, or any part or component of such a thing.

A person found guilty of the offences in this section is liable to the discretionary prohibition order prescribed by s. 110, unless the accused was prohibited from possessing weapons or other regulated items at the time of the offence, in which case the mandatory prohibition order in s. 109 applies.

Note mandatory forfeiture of weapons used in commission of an offence in s. 491.

SYNOPSIS

This section focuses on the circumstances under which the accused carries a weapon, prohibited device, ammunition or prohibited ammunition. If the accused has it while attending or on the way to a public meeting, the accused is guilty unless there is a lawful excuse for the possession of the weapon. An example of such an excuse would be that the accused is a peace officer armed in the line of duty (see s. 117.07). No additional intention, such as the intention to use the weapon, is required.

CARRYING CONCEALED WEAPON / Punishment.

90. (1) Every person commits an offence who carries a weapon, a prohibited device or any prohibited ammunition concealed, unless the person is authorized under the *Firearms Act* to carry it concealed.

(2) Every person who commits an offence under subsection (1)

    (a) is guilty of an indictable offence and liable to imprisonment for a term not exceeding five years; or

    (b) is guilty of an offence punishable on summary conviction. 1995, c. 39, s. 139.

in a criminal law context constitutes a breach of security of the person. They held that the breach of the principles of fundamental justice came about by the fact that the requirements of s. 287(4) permitting an abortion where it was approved by hospital committee while seemingly neutral on their face, resulted in abortions being absolutely unavailable in many areas and hospitals, and does not provide a clear legal standard to be applied by the therapeutic abortion committee in reaching its decision as to when to grant a certificate. One of the basic tenets of a criminal justice system is that when Parliament creates a defence to a criminal charge the defence should not be illusory or so difficult to attain as to be practically illusory. While Parliament must be given room to design an appropriate administrative and procedural structure for bringing into operation a particular defence to criminal liability, if that structure is too manifestly unfair, having regard to the decisions it is called upon to make, as to violate the principles of fundamental justice then the structure must be struck down. Beetz and Estey JJ. were of the view that the procedural requirements of s. 287, by significantly delaying a pregnant woman's access to medical treatment, result in additional dangers to her health and thereby deprive her of her rights to security of the person and do so in a manner which does not accord with the principles of fundamental justice. Finally Wilson J. held that the legislative scheme set up in s. 287 not only violates the pregnant woman's rights to security of the person but also the right to liberty as guaranteed by s. 7.

A statutory defence, like any other legislative provision, is not immune from scrutiny under the Charter. Further, there is no basis for the court adopting a position of strong deference in reviewing statutory defences such as compulsion under s. 17 of the *Criminal Code*: *R. v. Ruzic* (2001), 153 C.C.C. (3d) 1, 41 C.R. (5th) 1 (S.C.C.).

This section does not require that a defence such as drunkenness be available for all offences. Thus, it was open to Parliament in creating the offence of impaired driving to preclude drunkenness as a defence. The mental element of voluntary intoxication is a sufficiently guilty mind: *R. v. Penno*, [1990] 2 S.C.R. 865, 59 C.C.C. (3d) 344, 80 C.R. (3d) 97.

The principles of fundamental justice contemplate an accusatorial and adversarial system of criminal justice which is founded on respect for the autonomy and dignity of the person. These principles require that an accused, who is fit to stand trial, have the right to control his own defence. Any common law limit on this right which infringes the life, liberty or security of the person, must be the least intrusive rule which will attain the objectives which are of sufficient importance to override this section of the Charter: *R. v. Swain*, [1991] 1 S.C.R. 933, 63 C.C.C. (3d) 481, 5 C.R. (4th) 253.

Moral involuntariness is a principle of fundamental justice protected by this section. Only voluntary conduct being behaviour that is the product of a free will and controlled body unhindered by external constraints, should attract the penalty and stigma and criminal liability. The defence of compulsion by threats in s. 17 of the *Criminal Code* violates this section because the existence of certain requirements of the defence would allow for the conviction of an individual who acted involuntarily. Those requirements — immediacy (threat of immediate death or bodily harm) and presence (threat from a person who is present when the offence is committed) — infringe this section and must be struck down as unconstitutional: *R. v. Ruzic* (2001), 153 C.C.C. (3d) 1, 41 C.R. (5th) 1 (S.C.C.).

SEARCH OR SEIZURE.

8. Everyone has the right to be secure against unreasonable search or seizure.

ANNOTATIONS

Interpretation generally – Section 8 of the Charter limits the federal and provincial governments' powers of search and seizure. It does not, however, confer any power, even of reasonable search and seizure. These powers are grounded either in the common law or statute. To assess the constitutionality of a search and seizure, or of an authorizing statute, the court must focus on the reasonable or unreasonable impact on its subject, and not simply on its rationality in furtherance of a valid government objective. This section guarantees a

**EXAMPLE 2.2
WORDING OF
THE SECTION**

CHAPTER 3

The Criminal Code

Organization

Introduction

The *Criminal Code* is a federal statute that describes the elements of criminal offences in Canada. The Code also provides the procedure for processing criminal cases.

The building blocks of the Code are its sections and parts. The Code consists of sections 1 to 849 and groups the sections together by topic. These groups are referred to as parts, and the Code consists of 28 parts. Part XXVIII / Miscellaneous, which is the last part, lists all of the forms applicable to the Code: Forms 1 to 54.

Numbering System

Generally, Roman numerals indicate parts. For example, Part III is Firearms and Other Weapons.

Some parts have a Roman numeral followed by a decimal point and a standard number. For example, Part XII.2 is Proceeds of Crime. This form of numbering indicates that there was a legislative amendment, which means that Parliament passed a law that changed the Code. The legislature inserted Part XII.2 into the existing Code. (For further information on amendments and their effects on numbering, see Chapter 7 of this study guide.)

Standard numbers indicate sections—for example, section 16. An amendment may add, remove, or revise a section. When an amendment creates a new section that relates to the subject matter of an existing section, the new section has the same number as the existing section plus a decimal point and an added number. The same process applies to subsections, paragraphs, subparagraphs, and clauses.

Example 3.1

Review section 434 and section 434.1 (reproduced below) of the Code, which was added by Parliament after section 434. Section 434.1 refers specifically to "causes damage by fire or explosion to property."

First, section 434 provides the elements of the offence of arson where the person who committed arson does not own the damaged property. Second, section 434.1 further specifies the offence of arson where the person who committed arson owns the damaged property.

EXAMPLE 3.1
THE FIRST OF
TWO RELATED
SECTIONS

S. 434 MARTIN'S CRIMINAL CODE, 2020

ARSON / Damage to property.

434. Every person who intentionally or recklessly causes damage by fire or explosion to property that is not wholly owned by that person is guilty of an indictable offence and liable to imprisonment for a term not exceeding fourteen years. R.S., c. C-34, s. 390; 1990, c. 15, s. 1.

CROSS-REFERENCES

The term "property" is defined in s. 428. The term "recklessly" is not defined but reference might be made to *R. v. Sansregret*, [1985] 1 S.C.R. 570, 18 C.C.C. (3d) 223, where recklessness was defined as being found "in the attitude of one who, aware that there is danger that his conduct could bring about the result prohibited by the criminal law, nevertheless persists, despite the risk. It is, in other words, the conduct of one who sees the risk and who takes the chance." The defence of legal justification or excuse and colour of right is set out in s. 429(2).

This offence may be the basis for a conviction for constructive murder under s. 230.

Section 17 limits the availability of the statutory defence of compulsion by threats to the offence of "arson".

The accused may elect his mode of trial under s. 536(2). Release pending trial is determined under s. 515.

Related offences: s. 81, using explosives; s. 433, intentionally or recklessly causing damage by fire or explosion to property where bodily harm is caused or where person knows property is occupied; s. 434.1, intentionally or recklessly causing damage by fire or explosion to property wholly owned by accused; s. 435, causing damage by fire or explosion with intent to defraud; s. 436, causing fire or explosion through negligence; s. 436.1, possession of incendiary material.

SYNOPSIS

The section creates the offence of willfully or recklessly causing damage by fire or explosion to property that the accused does not wholly own. This is an indictable offence carrying a maximum sentence of 14 years.

ANNOTATIONS

This is a general intent offence for which intoxication falling short of automatism is not available as a defence. The *actus reus* is the damaging of property by fire. The mental element is the intentional or reckless performance of the illegal act. No additional knowledge or purpose is needed. In assessing the issue of intent, the trier of fact must consider all of the surrounding circumstances. The manner in which the fire started is likely to be an important consideration. Ultimately, the question is whether it can be inferred that the accused intended to damage someone else's property or was reckless whether damage ensued or not: *R. v. Tatton*, [2015] 2 S.C.R. 574, 323 C.C.C. (3d) 166.

The term "damage" does not require proof that the property was diminished in value by the fire. Damage may include physical harm to the property: *R. v. V. (M.)* (1998), 123 C.C.C. (3d) 138 (Ont. C.A.).

Recklessness requires proof that the accused actually knew that damage by fire to the property specified was the probable consequence of the proposed action and the accused proceeded with the conduct in the face of the risk. In this case, proof of intentional burning of a bag of chips, without knowledge of the probable consequence that the building would burn, was insufficient to establish the requisite *mens rea*: *R. v. D. (S.D.)* (2002), 164 C.C.C. (3d) 1 (Nfld. & Lab. C.A.).

ARSON / Own property.

434.1 Every person who intentionally or recklessly causes damage by fire or explosion to property that is owned, in whole or in part, by that person is guilty of an indictable offence and liable to imprisonment for a term not exceeding fourteen years, where the

EXAMPLE 3.1
A LATER
PROVISION
RELATED TO
SECTION 434

816

fire or explosion seriously threatens the health, safety or property of another person. 1990, c. 15, s. 1.

CROSS-REFERENCES

The term "property" is defined in s. 428. The term "recklessly" is not defined but reference might be made to *R. v. Sansregret*, [1985] 1 S.C.R. 570, 18 C.C.C. (3d) 223, where recklessness was defined as being found "in the attitude of one who, aware that there is danger that his conduct could bring about the result prohibited by the criminal law, nevertheless persists, despite the risk. It is, in other words, the conduct of one who sees the risk and who takes the chance." The defence of legal justification or excuse and colour of right is set out in s. 429(2).

Section 17 limits the availability of the statutory defence of compulsion by threats to the offence of "arson".

The accused may elect his mode of trial under s. 536(2). Release pending trial is determined under s. 515.

Related offences: s. 81, using explosives; s. 433, intentionally or recklessly causing damage by fire or explosion to property where bodily harm is caused or where person knows property is occupied; s. 434, intentionally or recklessly causing damage by fire or explosion to property not wholly owned by accused; s. 435, causing damage by fire or explosion with intent to defraud; s. 436, causing fire or explosion through negligence; s. 436.1, possession of incendiary material.

SYNOPSIS

The section creates the offence of willfully or recklessly causing damage by fire or explosion to property owned, in whole or in part, by the accused, where the fire or explosion *seriously threatens* the health, safety or property of *another person*. This is an indictable offence carrying a maximum sentence of 14 years.

ANNOTATIONS

The Crown is not required to prove that the accused knew that the fire threatened the health, safety, or property of others: *R. v. Bastien* (2017), 349 C.C.C. (3d) 149 (B.C.C.A.).

ARSON FOR FRAUDULENT PURPOSE / Holder or beneficiary of fire insurance policy.

435. (1) Every person who, with intent to defraud any other person, causes damage by fire or explosion to property, whether or not that person owns, in whole or in part, the property, is guilty of an indictable offence and liable to imprisonment for a term not exceeding ten years.

(2) Where a person is charged with an offence under subsection (1), the fact that the person was the holder of or was named as a beneficiary under a policy of fire insurance relating to the property in respect of which the offence is alleged to have been committed is a fact from which intent to defraud may be inferred by the court. R.S., c. C-34, s. 391; 1990, c. 15, s. 1.

CROSS-REFERENCES

The term "property" is defined in s. 428. Section 17 limits the availability of the statutory defence of compulsion by threats to the offence of "arson". The accused may elect his mode of trial under s. 536(2). Release pending trial is determined under s. 515.

Related offences: s. 81, using explosives; s. 433, intentionally or recklessly causing damage by fire or explosion to property where bodily harm is caused or where person knows property is occupied; s. 434, intentionally or recklessly causing damage by fire or explosion to property not wholly owned by accused; s. 434.1, intentionally or recklessly causing damage by fire or explosion to property wholly owned by accused; s. 436, causing fire or explosion through negligence; s. 436.1, possession of incendiary material.

The Code numbers forms in a similar way to numbering sections. For example, Form 5.1 indicates an amendment to Form 5.

Martin's Annual Criminal Code provides assistance to find a particular section. At the top of each page, you will find a section number, although it does not indicate all section numbers on that page. You will find the first section printed on the left-hand page. You will find the last section printed on the right-hand page. Similarly, following section 849 of the Code, you will find form numbers at the top of the page.

Parts, Topic Categories, and Sections

Generally, Part II through Part XIII describes the offences in the Code. Part XIV through Part XXVIII addresses criminal procedure, including Part XVI / Compelling Appearance of Accused Before a Justice and Interim Release and Part XXVII / Summary Convictions.

Each part of the Code groups the sections together according to their common characteristics. Within each part, headings identify topic categories. In the Table of Contents, each part lists headings in order of appearance.

Example 3.2

How do you find an offence if you do not know the section number? You can use either the Index or the Table of Contents to find it.

Review Part IX / Offences Against Rights of Property in the Table of Contents (reproduced below). The Table of Contents lists the types of offences in Part IX, which are also the topic categories under Part IX. Furthermore, the Table of Contents indicates the first page of a topic category.

Example 3.3

Part VIII / Offences Against the Person and Reputation includes the criminal offences that cause injury, death, or physical or psychological trauma to a person. The chart below lists some headings, topic categories, and sections in Part VIII.

Definitions

The Code starts with section 1, Short Title. Next, there are six sections grouped under the heading Interpretation. The sections are section 2, Definitions; 2.1, Further Definitions; 2.2, Acting on Victim's Behalf; 2.3, Concurrent Jurisdiction; 3, Descriptive Cross-References; and 3.1, Effect of Judicial Acts.

Section 2 provides the definitions that apply to the entire Code. The first words of section 2 are "In this Act." Therefore, every word or phrase defined in section 2 has that same meaning throughout the Code.

In contrast, definitions found elsewhere in the Code apply only to a particular part or section.

PART VIII.1 / OFFENCES RELATING TO CONVEYANCES 670
    Interpretation 670
    Recognition and Declaration 671
    Offences and Punishment 671
    Investigative Matters. 678
    Evidentiary Matters 682
    General Provisions 685

PART IX / OFFENCES AGAINST RIGHTS OF PROPERTY 686
    Interpretation 686
    Theft. 687
    Offences Resembling Theft. 701
    Robbery and Extortion 711
    Criminal Interest Rate. 720
    Breaking and Entering 724
    Possession and Trafficking 734
    False Pretences. 744
    Forgery and Offences Resembling Forgery. 749

PART X / FRAUDULENT TRANSACTIONS RELATING TO
CONTRACTS AND TRADE 760
    Interpretation 760
    Fraud. 760
    Falsification of Books and Documents 781
    Identity Theft and Identity Fraud 785
    Forgery of Trademarks and Trade Descriptions. 788
    Wreck. 792
    Public Stores 793
    Breach of Contract, Intimidation and Discrimination Against
        Trade Unionists 797
    Secret Commissions 803

PART XI / WILFUL AND FORBIDDEN ACTS IN RESPECT OF
CERTAIN PROPERTY 805
    Interpretation 805
    Mischief 807
    Arson and Other Fires 815
    Other Interference with Property 819
    Animals. 823
    Cruelty to Animals. 825

PART XII / OFFENCES RELATING TO CURRENCY 828
    Interpretation 828
    Making 829
    Possession 829

C / 4

**EXAMPLE 3.2
TOPIC
CATEGORIES
INDICATE PAGE
NUMBERS
RELATED TO
TYPES OF CODE
OFFENCES**

PART VIII / OFFENCES AGAINST THE PERSON AND REPUTATION

MURDER, MANSLAUGHTER AND INFANTICIDE

Murder, section 229
Murder Reduced to Manslaughter, section 232
Punishment for Murder, section 235

ASSAULTS

Assault with a Weapon or Causing Bodily Harm, section 267
Aggravated Assault, section 268
Disarming a Peace Officer, section 270.1
Sexual Assault, section 271

HATE PROPAGANDA

Advocating Genocide, section 318
Public Incitement of Hatred, section 319

**EXAMPLE 3.3
SOME HEADINGS,
TOPIC CATEGORIES,
AND SECTIONS IN
PART VIII**

EXERCISES

3.1   What part of the Code addresses sexual offences? (Hint: use the Table of Contents.)

_____
_____
_____
_____
_____

3.2   What is the section number at the top corner of the first page of the part that includes sexual offences?

_____
_____
_____
_____
_____

3.3   What is at the bottom corner of the same page?

_____
_____
_____
_____
_____

Example 3.4

Section 118 of the Code (reproduced below) is the first section in Part IV / Offences Against the Administration of Law and Justice. The first words of the section are "In this Part," followed by definitions of several words and phrases. These definitions only apply to Part IV.

The cross-references for section 118 indicate that it is necessary to refer back to section 2 of the Code for the definitions of other words and phrases that are used in Part IV.

Remember that some definitions apply only to the individual part, whereas other definitions apply to the entire Code.

S. 117.15   MARTIN'S CRIMINAL CODE, 2020

Amnesty period

(3) The amnesty period begins on the day on which this Order is registered and ends on February 28, 2021.

Coming into force

3. This Order comes into force on the day on which it is registered. **SOR/2018-46.**

REGULATIONS / Restriction/ Non-restricted firearm / Restricted firearm.

117.15 (1) Subject to subsection (2), the Governor in Council may make regulations prescribing anything that by this Part is to be or may be prescribed.

(2) In making regulations, the Governor in Council may not prescribe any thing to be a prohibited firearm, a restricted firearm, a prohibited weapon, a restricted weapon, a prohibited device or prohibited ammunition if, in the opinion of the Governor in Council, the thing to be prescribed is reasonable for use in Canada for hunting or sporting purposes.

(3) Despite the definitions "prohibited firearm" and "restricted firearm" in subsection 84(1), a firearm that is prescribed to be a non-restricted firearm is deemed not to be a prohibited firearm or a restricted firearm.

(4) Despite the definition "prohibited firearm" in subsection 84(1), a firearm that is prescribed to be a restricted firearm is deemed not to be a prohibited firearm.1995, c. 39, s. 139; 2015, c. 27, s. 34.

CROSS-REFERENCES
"Prohibited firearm", "restricted firearm", "non-restricted firearm", "prohibited weapon", "restricted weapon", "prohibited device" and "prohibited ammunition" are defined in s. 84(1). Publication of regulations is governed by the *Statutory Instruments Act*, R.S.C. 1985, c. S-22. A much wider regulation power is included in s. 117 of the *Firearms Act*.

SYNOPSIS
This section gives the Governor in Council the power to make regulations prescribing anything that may be prescribed under this part, for example, prohibited ammunition, prohibited device, prohibited firearm, prohibited weapon, restricted firearm and restricted weapon. However, subsec. (2) prevents the Governor in Council from prescribing anything as prohibited ammunition, prohibited device, prohibited firearm, prohibited weapon, restricted firearm and restricted weapon if the thing to be prescribed is reasonable for use in Canada for hunting or sporting purposes. Subsections (3) and (4), respectively, entail that, notwithstanding the definitions given in s. 84(1), no firearm prescribed to be a non-restricted firearm can be considered to be a prohibited firearm or a restricted firearm, and that no firearm prescribed to be a restricted firearm can be considered to be a prohibited firearm.

Part IV / OFFENCES AGAINST THE ADMINISTRATION OF LAW AND JUSTICE

Interpretation

DEFINITIONS / "Evidence" or "statement" / "Government" / "Judicial proceeding" / "Office" / "Official" / "Witness".

118. In this Part
"evidence" or "statement" means an assertion of fact, opinion, belief or knowledge, whether material or not and whether admissible or not;

252

EXAMPLE 3.4 APPLICATION OF DEFINITIONS

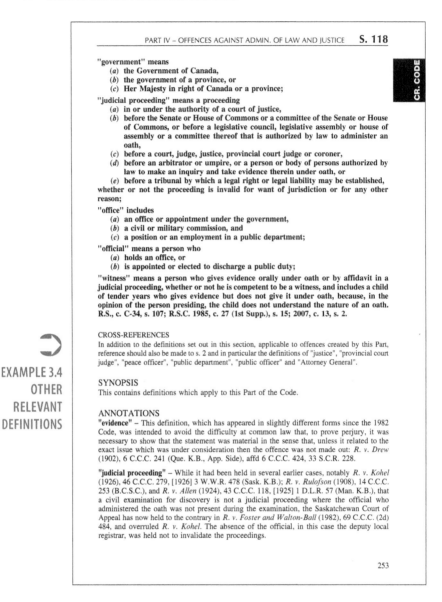

EXAMPLE 3.4
OTHER
RELEVANT
DEFINITIONS

PART IV – OFFENCES AGAINST ADMIN. OF LAW AND JUSTICE **S. 118**

CR. CODE

"government" means
   (a) the Government of Canada,
   (b) the government of a province, or
   (c) Her Majesty in right of Canada or a province;

"judicial proceeding" means a proceeding
   (a) in or under the authority of a court of justice,
   (b) before the Senate or House of Commons or a committee of the Senate or House of Commons, or before a legislative council, legislative assembly or house of assembly or a committee thereof that is authorized by law to administer an oath,
   (c) before a court, judge, justice, provincial court judge or coroner,
   (d) before an arbitrator or umpire, or a person or body of persons authorized by law to make an inquiry and take evidence therein under oath, or
   (e) before a tribunal by which a legal right or legal liability may be established,
whether or not the proceeding is invalid for want of jurisdiction or for any other reason;

"office" includes
   (a) an office or appointment under the government,
   (b) a civil or military commission, and
   (c) a position or an employment in a public department;

"official" means a person who
   (a) holds an office, or
   (b) is appointed or elected to discharge a public duty;

"witness" means a person who gives evidence orally under oath or by affidavit in a judicial proceeding, whether or not he is competent to be a witness, and includes a child of tender years who gives evidence but does not give it under oath, because, in the opinion of the person presiding, the child does not understand the nature of an oath. R.S., c. C-34, s. 107; R.S.C. 1985, c. 27 (1st Supp.), s. 15; 2007, c. 13, s. 2.

CROSS-REFERENCES
In addition to the definitions set out in this section, applicable to offences created by this Part, reference should also be made to s. 2 and in particular the definitions of "justice", "provincial court judge", "peace officer", "public department", "public officer" and "Attorney General".

SYNOPSIS
This contains definitions which apply to this Part of the Code.

ANNOTATIONS
"evidence" – This definition, which has appeared in slightly different forms since the 1982 Code, was intended to avoid the difficulty at common law that, to prove perjury, it was necessary to show that the statement was material in the sense that, unless it related to the exact issue which was under consideration then the offence was not made out: *R. v. Drew* (1902), 6 C.C.C. 241 (Que. K.B., App. Side), affd 6 C.C.C. 424, 33 S.C.R. 228.

"judicial proceeding" – While it had been held in several earlier cases, notably *R. v. Kohel* (1926), 46 C.C.C. 279, [1926] 3 W.W.R. 478 (Sask. K.B.); *R. v. Rulofson* (1908), 14 C.C.C. 253 (B.C.S.C.), and *R. v. Allen* (1924), 43 C.C.C. 118, [1925] 1 D.L.R. 57 (Man. K.B.), that a civil examination for discovery is not a judicial proceeding where the official who administered the oath was not present during the examination, the Saskatchewan Court of Appeal has now held to the contrary in *R. v. Foster and Walton-Ball* (1982), 69 C.C.C. (2d) 484, and overruled *R. v. Kohel*. The absence of the official, in this case the deputy local registrar, was held not to invalidate the proceedings.

253

Section 2 and other sections of the Code may define the same word. Which is the correct definition if there are multiple definitions of the same word?

Example 3.5

Section 2 and subsection 270.1(2), Definition of Weapon, define the word "weapon." A review of the two definitions reveals that the definition of "weapon" in subsection 270.1(2) is more specific and more restrictive than the section 2 definition.

The broader section 2 definition means

any thing used, designed to be used or intended for use
    (a) in causing death or injury to any person, or
    (b) for the purpose of threatening or intimidating any person
and, without restricting the generality of the foregoing, includes a firearm
and, for the purposes of sections 88, 267 and 272, any thing used, designed to
be used or intended for use in binding or tying up a person against their will.

The narrower subsection 270.1(2) definition means "any thing that is designed to be used to cause injury or death to, or to temporarily incapacitate, a person."

The subsection 270.1(2) definition of "weapon" only applies to section 270.1 and the offence it creates.

EXERCISES

3.4   When working with section 177 of the Code, Trespassing at Night, you will need to understand the meaning of "prowls at night." What is the definition of "night"? Identify the relevant section of the Code.

      _____

      _____

      _____

      _____

      _____

3.5   Where and how does the Code define "theft," "steal," and "robbery"? (Hint: use the Index.) Identify the relevant sections of the Code.

      _____

      _____

      _____

      _____

      _____

3.6   When working with section 348 of the Code, Breaking and Entering with Intent, Committing Offence or Breaking Out, you will need to understand the meaning of "break," "enter," and "place." Where are the definitions for these terms? Identify the relevant sections in the Code.

      _____

      _____

      _____

      _____

      _____

CHAPTER 4

Index

The Index guides readers to specific information in the *Canadian Charter of Rights and Freedoms* and other statutes included in *Martin's Annual Criminal Code*. Section numbers are used to direct readers to the correct location.

When the Index refers to a section of the *Criminal Code*, there are no initials preceding the section number. When the entry refers to a section of the Charter, the abbreviation "CH" precedes the section. The other statutes included in Martin's also have abbreviations. The editor's note at the top of page IN/1 lists the following:

CD = Controlled Drugs and Substances Act
CE = Canada Evidence Act
CH = Canadian Charter of Rights and Freedoms
WC = Crimes Against Humanity and War Crimes Act
YC = Youth Criminal Justice Act

General headings are capitalized, in bold type, and listed alphabetically. Many of these headings have several levels of subheadings. If you do not know the correct heading, the Index also provides cross-references to assist you.

Example 4.1

Your professor has asked you to determine the procedure required to obtain a telewarrant. Review the general heading "TELEWARRANTS" (reproduced below). The Index entry tells you to "*See*" two other general headings: "SEARCH AND SEIZURE" and "WARRANTS."

Review the general heading "SEARCH AND SEIZURE," where you will find a subheading, "Telewarrants." Under this subheading, topics include "formalities re warrant, 487.1(6)" and "proof of authorization, 487.1(11)," which refer to criminal procedures required to obtain a telewarrant. The references direct you to section 487.1 of the Code.

EXAMPLE 4.1 WHERE TO FIND INDEX ENTRIES FOR INFORMATION ON TELEWARRANTS

INDEX

TELECOMMUNICATION — *Continued*
Service or facility — *Continued*
  possession, etc., of device to obtain use of,
    327(1)
Theft of, 326(1)

TELEPHONE CALLS. *See also*
  INTERCEPTION OF PRIVATE
  COMMUNICATIONS
False messages, 372(1)
Harassing, 372(3)
Indecent, 372(2)
Number recorder warrant, 492.2

TELEWARRANTS. *See* SEARCH AND
  SEIZURE; WARRANTS

TERRITORIAL DIVISION. *See also*
  JURISDICTION—Territorial
Definition, 2

TERRITORIAL JURISDICTION. *See also*
  JURISDICTION—Territorial
Arrest, search or seizure, and other powers,
  477.3
Breach of probation, 733.1(2). *See also*
  BREACH OF PROBATION;
  SENTENCE—Probation
Consent of Attorney General for offences
  committed at sea, 477.2, 477.3(2)
Credit card offences, 342(2)
Defamatory libel, 478(2), (5)
Fishing zones, 477.1
Offence —
  aircraft in flight, in, 476(d)
  between territorial divisions, 476(a), (b)
  committed entirely in province, 478(1)
  continental shelf, in, above or beyond, 477.1
  elsewhere in province, 479
  mail being delivered, 476(e)
  not in a province, 481
  outside Canada, jurisdiction for commencing
    prosecution, 477.4(1)
  unorganized territory, in, 480
  vehicle or vessel, in, 476(c)
Ships, 477-477.4
Space station, 7(2.3)-(2.34)
Terrorism, 7(3.73)-(3.75)
Transfer of charges, 478, 479
Unorganized territory, 480
Warrant of arrest, 703. *See also*
  ARREST—Warrants

TERRITORIES. *See* NORTHWEST
  TERRITORIES; NUNAVUT; YUKON
  TERRITORY

TERRORISM
Attorney General of Canada may conduct
  prosecution, 83.25
Bail hearing, special conditions, 515(4.1)-(4.3)

TERRORISM — *Continued*
Consent of Attorney General —
  investigative hearing, 83.28(3)
  prosecution of breach of freezing provisions,
    83.24
  prosecution of terrorism offences, 83.24
  recognizance, 83.3(1), 810.011(1)
Consent of Attorney General of Canada —
  offence committed outside Canada by non-
    citizen, where, 7(7)
Definitions —
  Canadian, 83.01(1)
  entity, 83.01(1)
  listed entity, 83.01(1), 83.05
  terrorism offence, 2
  terrorist activity, 83.01(1)
    saving for mere expression, 83.01(1.1)
  terrorist group, 83.01(1)
Financing offences —
  Attorney General's consent to prosecution
    required, 83.24
  providing property for carrying out —
    intimidation of public etc., 83.02(b)
    terrorist activity, 83.02(a)
  providing property for terrorist purposes,
    83.03
  using property for terrorist purposes, 83.04
First degree murder, 231(6.01)
Forfeiture of property, 83.14, 83.15-83.17 *See
  also* OFFENCE-RELATED PROPERTY;
  PROCEEDS OF CRIME
Freezing property. *See also* OFFENCE-
  RELATED PROPERTY; PROCEEDS OF
  CRIME
  dealing in property of terrorist group
    prohibited, 83.08, 83.12
  disclosure of property of terrorist group,
    83.1, 83.11, 83.12
  Solicitor General may exempt person, 83.09
Hoax, 83.231
Interception of private communications, 183
  special provisions, 185(1.1), 186(1.1), 186.1,
    196
Investigative hearing, 83.28
  annual report, 83.31
  arrest warrant may issue, 83.29
  consent of Attorney General, 83.28(3)
  sunset clause, 83.32
  transition provision, 83.33
Listed entities —
  application for removal from list, 83.05(2)-
    (8)
  admission of confidential foreign
    information, 83.06
  certificate that not listed entity, 83.07
  defined, 83.01(1)
  Governor in Council may establish list, 83.05
  Solicitor General shall review list, 83.05(9)-
    (10)

INDEX

IN / 117

Review the general heading "WARRANTS." The entry under the subheading "Search Warrant" states, "*See* SEARCH AND SEIZURE – Warrants."

Most sections referenced in the Index are correct and current. However, the sections printed in bold italic type are no longer in effect or are not yet in effect.

Example 4.2

Your professor has asked you to check the Index for a section of the Code that is not yet in force or no longer in effect. This is indicated in Martin's by bolding and italicizing the section number, as explained in the introduction to the Index. Depending on the status of legislation at the time of publication, there may not be any status changes to flag in the Index.

INDEX

NOTE: All references are to sections of the *Criminal Code* unless preceded by the following abbreviations:

CD = Controlled Drugs and Substances Act
CE = Canada Evidence Act
CH = Canadian Charter of Rights and Freedoms
WC = Crimes Against Humanity and War Crimes Act
YC = Youth Criminal Justice Act

NOTE: *Italicized* **section numbers in bold type refer to section numbers that were not yet or no longer in effect when this index was published.**

Cross-references assist you to find a topic that is no longer in the Code. For example, although parties in the justice system refer to "bail," that term is not in the Code. So the Index entry under "BAIL" states "*See* JUDICIAL INTERIM RELEASE."

EXERCISES

4.1   What is the reference for the term "search warrant" in the Index?

_____

_____

_____

_____

4.2   What is a "reasonable" search warrant? Is there an entry for "reasonable search and seizure"? What are the references? Where will you find them?

_____

_____

_____

_____

CHAPTER 5

Offence Grid

Introduction

The Offence Grid is located near the end of the book at the tab named "GRID." The page numbers start with the abbreviation "OG."

The Offence Grid is a chart that provides sentencing information and criminal procedure for each substantive offence created by the *Criminal Code*. Readers can use it to determine whether a particular sentence or judicial order applies to an offence.

Below, you will find the first page of the Offence Grid.

The Offence Grid summarizes information about Code offences. In particular, it provides:

- the type of offence (indictable, summary, or hybrid)
- the offences that are the absolute jurisdiction of the provincial court
- the maximum and minimum sentences
- the available sentences
- the illegal sentences and
- the discretionary and mandatory judicial orders.

Pages OG/1 and OG/2 include the Editor's Note, Disclaimer, Caution, and Note.

Type of Offence

The Code classifies offences into three types: indictable, summary, and hybrid. The offence classification determines the court processes for the Crown and the accused.

Indictable Offences

Indictable offences are the most serious criminal offences. Indictable offences listed in section 469 of the Code include aggravated sexual assault and murder. Indictable offence trials at a superior court of criminal jurisdiction include a judge and a jury. However, with the consent of the accused and the Attorney General, there may be a trial before a superior court judge without a jury.

THE FIRST PAGE OF THE OFFENCE GRID

OFFENCE GRID

Section	Type	Max/Min Sentence	Discharge s.730	Suspended Sentence s.731(1)(a)	Fine Alone s.734	Fine & Probation s.731(1)(b)	Prison & Probation s.731(1)(b)	Prison & Probation s.732.1(b)	Prison Fine s.734	Intermittent s.732	Fine, Prob. & Intermit. s.732	Conditional Sentence s.742.1	Comments (applicability depends on circumstances of case)
56.1 Procure etc. identity documents	Hyb-Ind.	5 yrs	✓	✓	✓	✓	✓	✓	✓	✓	✓		S if by indictment
	Hyb-Sum.	6 mth/5000*	✓	✓	✓	✓	✓	✓	✓	✓	✓	
57(1) Forge passport or use forged passport	Indictable	14 yrs	✗	✓	✓	✓	✓	✓	✓	✓	✗	S
57(2) Passport, false statement	Hyb-Ind.	2 yrs	✓	✓	✓	✓	✓	✓	✓	✓	✓	
	Hyb-Sum.	6 mth/5000*	✓	✓	✓	✓	✓	✓	✓	✓	✓	
57(3) Possession, forged passport	Indictable	5 yrs	✓	✓	✓	✓	✓	✓	✓	✓	✓	S
58 Fraud, use of citizenship certificate	Indictable	2 yrs	✓	✓	✓	✓	✓	✓	✓	✓	✓	
65(1) Riot	Indictable	2 yrs	✓	✓	✓	✓	✓	✓	✓	✓	✓	
65(2) Riot while masked	Indictable	10 yrs	✓	✓	✓	✓	✓	✓	✓	✓	✓	S
66(1) Unlawful assembly	Summary	6 mth/5000*	✓	✓	✓	✓	✓	✓	✓	✓	✓	
66(2) Unlawful assembly while masked	Hyb-Ind.	5 yrs	✓	✓	✓	✓	✓	✓	✓	✓	✓	S. 110 discretionary firearms order. S if by indictment
	Hyb-Sum.	6 mth/5000	✓	✓	✓	✓	✓	✓	✓	✓	✓	
72, 73 Forcible entry	Hyb-Ind.	2 yrs	✓	✓	✓	✓	✓	✓	✓	✓	✓	S. 110 discretionary firearms order.
	Hyb-Sum.	6 mth/5000*	✓	✓	✓	✓	✓	✓	✓	✓	✓	
75 Piratical acts	Indictable	14 yrs	✗	✓	✓	✓	✓	✓	✓	✓	✓	P
76 Hijacking	Indictable	Life	✗	✓	✓	✓	✓	✓	✓	✓	✗	P S. 109 mandatory firearms order.
77 Endanger aircraft	Indictable	Life	✗	✓	✓	✓	✓	✓	✓	✓	✗	P S. 109 mandatory firearms order.
78 Take weapon or explosive on board	Indictable	14 yrs	✗	✓	✓	✓	✓	✓	✓	✓	✗	S. 109 mandatory firearms order. S. 491 mandatory weapon forfeiture order. S
78.1 Seizing control of ship etc.	Indictable	Life	✗	✓	✓	✓	✓	✓	✓	✓	✗	S. 109 mandatory firearms order. P

* $100,000 for organizations for summary conviction offence s.735.
*** conditional sentence not available if offence involved use of a weapon.

✓ Sentence Option ✗ Illegal Sentence

P = Primary designated offence
S = Secondary designated offence
PC = Primary Compulsory
[see note on p. OG/2]

GRID

OG/5

Section 2 of the Code defines the "superior court of criminal jurisdiction." The provinces and territorial governments select the name of the superior court, which includes the Court of Appeal, Superior Court of Justice, Superior Court, Supreme Court, Court of Queen's Bench, and Nunavut Court of Justice. Section 469 of the Code is reproduced below.

For most other indictable offences, the accused may elect the mode of trial. The accused must choose between trial by a provincial court judge, trial by a superior court judge alone, or trial by a superior court judge and jury.

S. 469 MARTIN'S CRIMINAL CODE, 2020

ANNOTATIONS

A superior court of criminal jurisdiction has the right to try those offences within the absolute jurisdiction of a provincial court judge: *R. v. Holliday* (1973), 12 C.C.C. (2d) 56, [1973] 5 W.W.R. 363 (Alta. S.C. App. Div.).

COURT OF CRIMINAL JURISDICTION / Accessories / Corrupting justice / Attempts / Conspiracy.

469. Every court of criminal jurisdiction has jurisdiction to try an indictable offence other than

- (*a*) **an offence under any of the following sections:**
  - (i) **section 47 (treason),**
  - (ii) **[*Repealed*, 2018, c. 29, s. 61.]**
  - (iii) **section 51 (intimidating Parliament or a legislature),**
  - (iv) **section 53 (inciting to mutiny),**
  - (v) **section 61 (seditious offences),**
  - (vi) **section 74 (piracy),**
  - (vii) **section 75 (piratical acts), or**
  - (viii) **section 235 (murder);**
- (*b*) **the offence of being an accessory after the fact to high treason or treason or murder;**
- (*c*) **an offence under section 119 (bribery) by the holder of a judicial office;**
- (*c*.1) **an offence under any of sections 4 to 7 of the *Crimes Against Humanity and War Crimes Act*;**
- (*d*) **the offence of attempting to commit any offence mentioned in subparagraphs (*a*)(i) to (vii); or**
- (*e*) **the offence of conspiring to commit any offence mentioned in paragraph (*a*).**
  R.S., c. C-34, s. 427; 1972, c. 13, s. 33; 1974-75-76, c. 93, s. 37, c. 105, s. 29; R.S.C. 1985, c. 27 (1st Supp.), s. 62; 2000, c. 24, s. 44; 2018, c. 29, s. 61.

C

SUPERIOR COURT OF CRIMINAL JURISDICTION OFFENCES LISTED IN THE CODE

CROSS-REFERENCES

Note that s. 3 provides that the descriptions in parenthesis after the section number are inserted for convenience of reference only and are no part of the provision.

The term "court of criminal jurisdiction" is defined in s. 2. Only the superior court of criminal jurisdiction has jurisdiction to try the offences listed in this section. As well, only a judge of the superior court of criminal jurisdiction may release an accused pending trial for these offences, by virtue of s. 522. The ordinary mode of trial for these offences is by virtue of the combined effect of ss. 468 and 471, by way of jury. However, provision is made for re-election for trial by judge alone under s. 473.

As to mode of trial generally, see the note under s. 468.

ANNOTATIONS

Neither the superior court of criminal jurisdiction nor the court of criminal jurisdiction have jurisdiction to try a summary conviction offence *ab initio: R. v. Rahim* (1977), 36 C.C.C. (2d) 533 (Ont. Co. Ct.).

JURISDICTION OVER PERSON.

470. Subject to this Act, every superior court of criminal jurisdiction and every court of criminal jurisdiction that has power to try an indictable offence is competent to try an accused for that offence

- (*a*) **if the accused is found, is arrested or is in custody within the territorial jurisdiction of the court; or**
- (*b*) **if the accused has been ordered to be tried by**

888

Some specific offences fall within the absolute jurisdiction of a provincial court judge. The Offence Grid identifies offences under section 553 of the Code by the notation "Absolute PCJ" in bold print in the "Type" column.

These "absolute jurisdiction" offences are listed in section 553 of the Code, reproduced below.

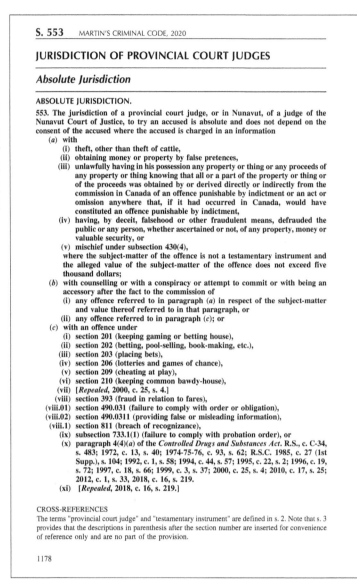

S. 553   MARTIN'S CRIMINAL CODE, 2020

JURISDICTION OF PROVINCIAL COURT JUDGES

Absolute Jurisdiction

ABSOLUTE JURISDICTION.

553. The jurisdiction of a provincial court judge, or in Nunavut, of a judge of the Nunavut Court of Justice, to try an accused is absolute and does not depend on the consent of the accused where the accused is charged in an information

(a) with
  (i) theft, other than theft of cattle,
  (ii) obtaining money or property by false pretences,
  (iii) unlawfully having in his possession any property or thing or any proceeds of any property or thing knowing that all or a part of the property or thing or of the proceeds was obtained by or derived directly or indirectly from the commission in Canada of an offence punishable by indictment or an act or omission anywhere that, if it had occurred in Canada, would have constituted an offence punishable by indictment,
  (iv) having, by deceit, falsehood or other fraudulent means, defrauded the public or any person, whether ascertained or not, of any property, money or valuable security, or
  (v) mischief under subsection 430(4),
  where the subject-matter of the offence is not a testamentary instrument and the alleged value of the subject-matter of the offence does not exceed five thousand dollars;
(b) with counselling or with a conspiracy or attempt to commit or with being an accessory after the fact to the commission of
  (i) any offence referred to in paragraph (a) in respect of the subject-matter and value thereof referred to in that paragraph, or
  (ii) any offence referred to in paragraph (c); or
(c) with an offence under
  (i) section 201 (keeping gaming or betting house),
  (ii) section 202 (betting, pool-selling, book-making, etc.),
  (iii) section 203 (placing bets),
  (iv) section 206 (lotteries and games of chance),
  (v) section 209 (cheating at play),
  (vi) section 210 (keeping common bawdy-house),
  (vii) [Repealed, 2000, c. 25, s. 4.]
  (viii) section 393 (fraud in relation to fares),
  (viii.01) section 490.031 (failure to comply with order or obligation),
  (viii.02) section 490.0311 (providing false or misleading information),
  (viii.1) section 811 (breach of recognizance),
  (ix) subsection 733.1(1) (failure to comply with probation order), or
  (x) paragraph 4(4)(a) of the Controlled Drugs and Substances Act. R.S., c. C-34, s. 483; 1972, c. 13, s. 40; 1974-75-76, c. 93, s. 62; R.S.C. 1985, c. 27 (1st Supp.), s. 104; 1992, c. 1, s. 58; 1994, c. 44, s. 57; 1995, c. 22, s. 2; 1996, c. 19, s. 72; 1997, c. 18, s. 66; 1999, c. 3, s. 37; 2000, c. 25, s. 4; 2010, c. 17, s. 25; 2012, c. 1, s. 33, 2018, c. 16, s. 219.
  (xi) [Repealed, 2018, c. 16, s. 219.]

CROSS-REFERENCES

The terms "provincial court judge" and "testamentary instrument" are defined in s. 2. Note that s. 3 provides that the descriptions in parenthesis after the section number are inserted for convenience of reference only and are no part of the provision.

1178

"ABSOLUTE JURISDICTION" OFFENCES LISTED IN THE CODE

Example 5.1

Turn to page OG/17 of the Offence Grid, reproduced below, and find the twelfth offence listed. In the first (left) column, you will find the section number for the offence with a description of the prohibited conduct of the offence. For example, the description for section 193.1 of the Code is "Disclosure of information, radio-based telephone communications." The next (right) column is the type of offence; in this case, the type is "indictable." The Offence Grid informs you that for an offence under section 193.1 of the Code, the accused may elect the mode of trial.

OFFENCE GRID

SECTION	TYPE	MAX/MIN SENTENCE	DISCHARGE s. 730	SUSPENDED SENTENCE s. 731(1)(a)	FINE ALONE s. 734	FINE & PROBATION s. 731(1)(b)	PRISON ss. 718.3, 787	PRISON & PROBATION s. 731(1)(b)	INTERMITTENT s. 732	FINE, PROB. & INTERMIT s. 732	CONDITIONAL SENTENCE s. 742.1	COMMENTS (applicability depends on circumstances of case)
176(1) Obstructing or violence to clergy	Indictable	2 yrs	✓	✓	✓	✓	✓	✓	✓	✓	✓	S. 110 discretionary firearms order. S. 491 mandatory weapon forfeiture order.
176(2) & (3) Disturbing religious worship, etc.	Summary	6 mth/ 5000*	✓	✓	✓	✓	✓	✓	✓	✓	✓	
177 Trespassing at night	Summary	6 mth/ 5000*	✓	✓	✓	✓	✓	✓	✓	✓	✓	
178 Offensive volatile substance	Summary	6 mth/ 5000*	✓	✓	✓	✓	✓	✓	✓	✓	✓	
179 Vagrancy	Summary	6 mth/ 5000*	✓	✓	✓	✓	✓	✓	✓	✓	✓	
180 Common nuisance	Indictable	2 yrs	✓	✓	✓	✓	✓	✓	✓	✓	✓	S. 110 discretionary firearms order. S. 491 mandatory weapon forfeiture order.
182 Dead body	Indictable	5 yrs	✓	✓	✓	✓	✓	✓	✓	✓	✓	S
184 Interception of communications	Indictable	5 yrs max	✓	✓	✓	✓	✓	✓	✓	✓	✓	S
184.5 Interception of radio-based telephone communications	Indictable	5 yrs max	✓	✓	✓	✓	✓	✓	✓	✓	✓	S
191 Possession, etc. of device for surreptitious interception of private communications	Indictable	2 yrs	✓	✓	✓	✓	✓	✓	✓	✓	✓	S. 192 discretionary forfeiture order.
193 Disclosure of information	Indictable	2 yrs	✓	✓	✓	✓	✓	✓	✓	✓	✓	S. 194 discretionary order of punitive damages to maximum of $5,000 on application of person aggrieved.
193.1 Disclosure of information, radio-based telephone communications	Indictable	2 yrs	✓	✓	✓	✓	✓	✓	✓	✓	✓	S. 194 discretionary order of punitive damages to maximum of $5,000 on application of person aggrieved.
201(1) Keeping gaming or betting house	Indictable **Absolute PCJ**	2 yrs	✓	✓	✓	✓	✓	✓	✓	✓	✓	S. 462.37 proceeds of crime forfeiture order on Crown application.
201(2) Person found in gaming or betting house or owner permitting use	Summary	6 mth/5000	✓	✓	✓	✓	✓	✓	✓	✓	✓	

* $100,000 for organizations for summary conviction offence s. 735.
*** conditional sentence not available if offence involved use of a weapon.

✓ Sentence Option   [X] Illegal Sentence

P = Primary designated offence
S = Secondary designated offence
PC = Primary Compulsory
[see note on p. OG/2]

EXAMPLE 5.1 SUMMARY, INDICTABLE, AND "ABSOLUTE JURISDICTION" OFFENCES

GRID

OG/17

The next offence listed is subsection 201(1), "Keeping gaming or betting house." Again, the type is "indictable"; however, the additional notation, "Absolute PCJ," in bold print indicates that for a subsection 201(1) offence, a provincial court judge must conduct the trial.

Section 553 of the Code also affects arrest procedures, particularly an arrest without warrant by a peace officer under subsection 495(2) of the Code. In general circumstances, according to paragraph 495(2)(a) of the Code, a peace officer shall not arrest a person without a warrant for an indictable offence listed in section 553 of the Code. Indictable offences include hybrid offences according to paragraph 34(1)(a) of the *Interpretation Act*, R.S.C. 1985, c. I-21. Therefore, a peace officer shall not arrest without a warrant a person accused of fraud in relation to fares under section 393(1) of the Code or mischief under section 430(4) of the Code.

In specific circumstances, a peace officer may arrest a person without a warrant for an indictable offence listed under section 553 of the Code. Subsection 495(2) of the Code provides criteria whereby a peace officer may arrest a person who is alleged to have committed a criminal offence listed under section 553 of the Code. More particularly, a peace officer who satisfies one of the following conditions may arrest an accused:

1. Under subsection 495(2)(d), a peace officer may arrest a person to protect the public, to protect property, to protect the accused, or to prevent a breach of the peace.
2. Under subparagraph 495(2)(d)(i), a peace officer may arrest a person to establish the person's identity.
3. Under subparagraph 495(2)(d)(ii), a peace officer may arrest a person to secure or preserve evidence of or relating to the criminal offence.
4. Under subparagraph 495(2)(d)(iii), a peace officer may arrest a person to prevent the repetition or continuation of the criminal offence or to prevent the commission of another criminal offence.
5. Under paragraph 495(2)(e), a peace officer may arrest a person to ensure that the accused attends court.

Nevertheless, even if any of the criteria under paragraph 495(2)(d) or 495(2)(e) are satisfied by a peace officer, the peace officer may still choose not to arrest an accused.

Importantly, an arrest made without a warrant, outside Code authority, is an unlawful arrest. First, the unlawful arrest may breach an accused's rights under the *Canadian Charter of Rights and Freedoms*. Second, an unlawful arrest may jeopardize the successful prosecution of the accused. Third, an unlawful arrest may lead to civil litigation brought against the arresting officer and his or her employer.

Summary Conviction Offences

A summary conviction offence is a minor criminal offence in which a judge, without a jury, conducts the trial. An example of a summary conviction offence is subsection 201(2) of the Code on page OG/17, reproduced above.

Hybrid Offences

Hybrid offences or dual procedure offences may follow either the procedure for indictable offences or the procedure for summary convictions. The Crown attorney will choose to prosecute either by indictment or by summary conviction procedure. However, according to paragraph 34(1)(a) of the *Interpretation Act*, a hybrid offence is indictable until the Crown elects to proceed by a summary conviction procedure. The Crown attorney's choice determines the trial procedure available to the accused. The Crown attorney's election also determines the sentences available following the conviction of an accused.

Example 5.2

Find section 270 of the Code, "Assault officer, resist arrest, etc.," on page OG/27 (reproduced below). In the "Type" column, you will find the notations "Hyb-Ind." and "Hyb-Sum." These notations confirm that the Crown can elect to prosecute either by indictment or by summary procedure.

OFFENCE GRID

SECTION	TYPE	MAX/MIN SENTENCE	DISCHARGE s. 730	SUSPENDED SENTENCE s. 731(1)(a)	FINE ALONE s. 734	FINE & PROBATION s. 731(1)(b)	PRISON & FINE ss. 718.3, 787	PRISON & PROBATION s. 731(1)(b)	INTERMITTENT s. 732	FINE, PROB. & INTERMIT. s. 732	CONDITIONAL SENTENCE s. 742.1	COMMENTS (applicability depends on circumstances of case)
268 Aggravated assault	Indictable	14 yrs	✗	✓	✓	✓	✓	✓	✓	✓	✗	S. 109 mandatory firearms order. S. 491 mandatory weapon forfeiture order. PC
269 Unlawfully cause bodily harm	Hyb-Ind.	10 yrs	✓	✓	✓	✓	✓	✓	✓	✓	✗	Indictable, s. 109 mandatory firearms order. Summary conviction, s. 110 discretionary firearms order. S. 491 mandatory weapon forfeiture order. May be convicted notwithstanding that charge.
	Hyb-Sum.	18 mth/ 5000*	✓	✓	✓	✓	✓	✓	✓	✓	✓	PC
269.1 Torture	Indictable	14 yrs	✗	✓	✓	✓	✓	✓	✓	✓	✗	S. 109 mandatory firearms order. S. 491 mandatory weapon forfeiture order. S
270 Assault officer, resist arrest, etc.	Hyb-Ind.	5 yrs	✓	✓	✓	✓	✓	✓	✓	✓	✓	S. 110 discretionary firearms order. S. 491 mandatory weapon forfeiture order.
	Hyb-Sum.	6 mth/ 5000*	✓	✓	✓	✓	✓	✓	✓	✓	✓	S
270.01 Assaulting peace officer with weapon or causing bodily harm	Hyb-Ind.	10 yrs	✓	✓	✓	✓	✓	✓	✓	✓	✗	S. 109 mandatory firearms order. S. 491 mandatory weapon forfeiture order. PC
	Hyb-Sum.	18 mth	✓	✓	✓	✓	✓	✓	✓	✓	✓	
270.02 Aggravated assault of peace officer	Indictable	14 yrs	✗	✓	✓	✓	✓	✓	✓	✓	✗	S. 109 mandatory firearms order. PC
270.1 Disarming peace officer	Hyb-Ind.	5 yrs	✓	✓	✓	✓	✓	✓	✓	✓	✓	S. 110 discretionary firearms order. S if by indictment
	Hyb-Sum.	18 mth	✓	✓	✓	✓	✓	✓	✓	✓	✓	

* $100,000 for organizations for summary conviction offence s. 735.
*** conditional sentence not available if offence involved use of a weapon.

✓ Sentence Option   ✗ Illegal Sentence

P = Primary designated offence
S = Secondary designated offence
PC = Primary Compulsory
[see note on p. OG/2]

EXAMPLE 5.2
HYBRID
OFFENCE

GRID

OG / 27

5.1 What type of offence is "trespassing at night"? (If you are unsure of the section number, find it in the Index.)

_____

_____

_____

_____

_____

5.2 What type of offence is "aggravated assault"?

_____

_____

_____

_____

5.3 What type of offence is "theft $5,000 or less"?

_____

_____

_____

_____

_____

5.4 A store security guard saw a suspect leaving a store with toothpaste in her pocket, for which she had not paid. The security guard apprehended the suspect after she walked out the door and called the police. Can the police officer arriving on the scene arrest the suspect for "theft $5,000 or less" without a warrant?

_____

_____

_____

_____

_____

5.5 Would the answer to Exercise 5.4 differ if the suspect was not carrying identification?

_____

_____

_____

_____

_____

Maximum/Minimum Sentence

The third column of the Offence Grid provides either the maximum sentence or the minimum and maximum sentences. For many offences, there is no minimum sentence; therefore, the column only provides the maximum sentence. Exceptions include the minimum sentences for various weapons offences, certain offences resulting in death, and a number of repeat offences.

MARTIN'S CRIMINAL CODE, 2020

SECTION / TYPE	MAX/MIN SENTENCE	DISCHARGE s. 730	SUSPENDED SENTENCE s. 731(1)(a)	FINE ALONE s. 734	FINE & PROBATION s. 731(1)(b)	PRISON s. 743.1-747	PRISON & PROBATION s. 731(1)(b)	PRISON & FINE s. 734	INTERMITTENT s. 732	FINE, PROB. & INTERMIT. s. 732	CONDITIONAL SENTENCE s. 742.1	COMMENTS
83.23(1)(b) Harbouring terrorist, carried out terrorism offence liable to any other punishment — Indictable	10 yrs	✓	✓	✓	✓	✓	✓	✓	✓	✓	✗	S. 83.26 sentence must be consecutive to any other imposed. P
83.231(2) Terrorist activity, hoax — Hyb-Ind.	5 yrs	✓	✓	✓	✓	✓	✓	✓	✓	✓	✓	S
Hyb-Sum.	6 mth/ 5000*	✓	✓	✓	✓	✓	✓	✓	✓	✓	✓	
83.231(3) Terrorism, hoax causing bodily harm — Hyb-Ind.	10 yrs	✓	✓	✓	✓	✓	✓	✓	✓	✓	✗	S. 110 discretionary firearms order. S
Hyb-Sum.	18 mth	✓	✓	✓	✓	✓	✓	✓	✓	✓	✓	
83.231(4) Terrorist hoax, causing death — Indictable	Life	✗	✓	✓	✓	✓	✓	✓	✓	✓	✗	S. 110 discretionary firearms order. S
85 Use of firearm or imitation, commission of offence — Indictable	14 yrs max. Minimums: 1 yr-1st 3 yrs-2nd	✗	✗	✗	✗	✓	**	✓	✗	✗	✗	S. 109 mandatory firearms order. S. 491 mandatory weapon forfeiture order. Sentence must be consecutive to any other imposed. **Not a possible sentence for a second offence because there is a minimum sentence of three years. Higher penalty for second or subsequent offence requires compliance with s. 727. S
86 Firearm, careless use or storage, breach of regulations — Hyb-Ind.	Maximums: 2 yrs-1st 5 yrs-2nd	✓	✓	✓	✓	✓	✓	✓	✓	✓	✓	S. 110 discretionary firearms order. S. 491 mandatory weapon forfeiture order. Higher penalty for second or subsequent offence requires compliance with s. 665.
Hyb-Sum.	6 mth/ 5000*	✓	✓	✓	✓	✓	✓	✓	✓	✓	✓	S (for secondary or subsequent offence if indictable)
87 Firearm, pointing — Hyb-Ind.	5 yrs	✓	✓	✓	✓	✓	✓	✓	✓	✓	✓	S. 110 discretionary firearms order. S. 491 mandatory weapon forfeiture order. S if by indictment
Hyb-Sum.	6 mth/ 5000*	✓	✓	✓	✓	✓	✓	✓	✓	✓	✓	
88 Possession for purpose dangerous to the public — Hyb-Ind.	10 yrs	✓	✓	✓	✓	✓	✓	✓	✓	✓	*** ✗	S. 109 mandatory firearms order. S. 491 mandatory weapon forfeiture order.
Hyb-Sum.	6 mth/ 5000*	✓	✓	✓	✓	✓	✓	✓	✓	✓	✓	S. 110 discretionary firearms order. S. 491 mandatory weapon forfeiture order. S if by indictment
89 Weapon at public meeting — Summary	6 mth/ 5000*	✓	✓	✓	✓	✓	✓	✓	✓	✓	✓	S. 110 discretionary firearms order. S. 491 mandatory weapon forfeiture order.

* $100,000 for organizations for summary conviction offence s. 735.
*** conditional sentence not available if offence involved use of a weapon.

✓ Sentence Option   ✗ Illegal Sentence

P = Primary designated offence
S = Secondary designated offence
PC = Primary Compulsory
[see note on p. OG/2]

OG / 8

EXAMPLE 5.3
MINIMUM
SENTENCE

Example 5.3

Find section 85 of the Code, "Use of firearm or imitation, commission of offence," on page OG/8 (reproduced above). In the "Max/Min Sentence" column, you will find the notations "Minimums: 1 yr-1st" and "3 yrs-2nd." These notations confirm that there is a mandatory minimum sentence. On the first offence, the minimum sentence is one year in custody. On the second offence, the minimum sentence is three years in custody.

There is a wide variation in the maximum sentences provided for hybrid offences depending upon whether the Crown attorney proceeds by indictment or by summary conviction procedure. For example, section 270 of the Code is a hybrid offence (reproduced below). For the indictable procedure, the maximum sentence is imprisonment for five years, whereas for the summary conviction procedure, the maximum sentence is two years less a day, a fine of $5,000, or both. The sentence is the general sentence for summary conviction offences under section 787 of the Code.

If the maximum sentence for an offence is imprisonment for five years or a longer period of incarceration, the accused has the right to choose a jury trial, according to paragraph 11(f) of the Charter.

Available Sentences

The ten columns to the right of the "Max/Min Sentence" column provide the available sentences for each offence. A check mark indicates that the sentence is available for the offence. There may be specific circumstances that limit each available sentence; the offence section of the Code provides those circumstances.

Discharge

Section 730 of the Code, Conditional and Absolute Discharge, provides the court with available sentences that allow the accused to avoid a criminal record. Pursuant to section 6.1 of the *Criminal Records Act*, R.S.C. 1985, c. C-47, a person who receives a discharge for an offence does not have to apply for a pardon from the National Parole Board. The person will have his or her record automatically destroyed. Thus, a discharge is beneficial to the accused.

A discharge is an available sentence if there is a finding of guilt at trial or if the accused pleads guilty. Although a "conviction" must be recorded for some offences, for other offences, a conviction is discretionary and a discharge is an option.

Example 5.4

Find section 268 of the Code, "Aggravated assault," on page OG/27 of the Offence Grid (reproduced below). The "X" found in the black box in column 4 indicates that a discharge pursuant to section 730 of the Code is not available. Consequently, the entry of a conviction on the record is mandatory. Section 730 of the Code (reproduced below) specifies when a discharge is not an available sentence. It is not an available sentence for offences where the maximum sentence is 14 years of imprisonment or imprisonment for life. Furthermore, a discharge is not available for an offence with a mandatory minimum sentence of incarceration.

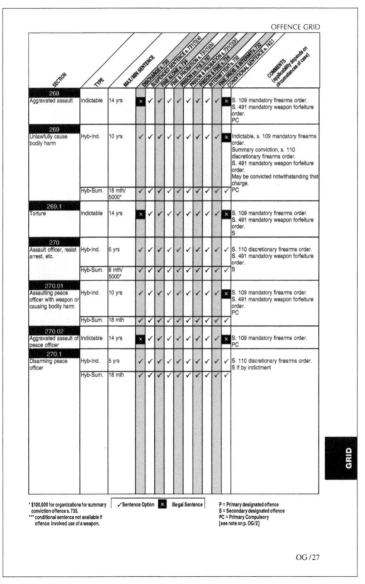

EXAMPLE 5.4
DISCHARGE IS NOT
AN AVAILABLE
SENTENCE

CR. CODE

(3) No certificate shall be admitted in evidence unless the party intending to produce it has, before the trial or hearing, as the case may be, given reasonable notice and a copy of the certificate to the party against whom it is to be produced.

(4) The party against whom a certificate of an analyst is produced may, with leave of the court, require the attendance of the analyst for cross-examination. 2011, c. 7, s. 2; 2018, c. 21, s. 23.

EXAMPLE 5.4
EXCLUSION OF
DISCHARGE AS AN
AVAILABLE
SENTENCE

Absolute and Conditional Discharges

CONDITIONAL AND ABSOLUTE DISCHARGE / Period for which appearance notice, etc., continues in force / Effect of discharge / Where person bound by probation order convicted of offence.

730. (1) Where an accused, other than an organization, pleads guilty to or is found guilty of an offence, other than an offence for which a minimum punishment is prescribed by law or an offence punishable by imprisonment for fourteen years or for life, the court before which the accused appears may, if it considers it to be in the best interests of the accused and not contrary to the public interest, instead of convicting the accused, by order direct that the accused be discharged absolutely or on the conditions prescribed in a probation order made under subsection 731(2).

(2) Subject to Part XVI, where an accused who has not been taken into custody or who has been released from custody under or by virtue of any provision of Part XVI pleads guilty of or is found guilty of an offence but is not convicted, the appearance notice, promise to appear, summons, undertaking or recognizance issued to or given or entered into by the accused continues in force, subject to its terms, until a disposition in respect of the accused is made under subsection (1) unless, at the time the accused pleads guilty or is found guilty, the court, judge or justice orders that the accused be taken into custody pending such a disposition.

(3) Where a court directs under subsection (1) that an offender be discharged of an offence, the offender shall be deemed not to have been convicted of the offence except that

    (a) the offender may appeal from the determination of guilt as if it were a conviction in respect of the offence;

    (b) the Attorney General and, in the case of summary conviction proceedings, the informant or the informant's agent may appeal from the decision of the court not to convict the offender of the offence as if that decision were a judgment or verdict of acquittal of the offence or a dismissal of the information against the offender; and

    (c) the offender may plead autrefois convict in respect of any subsequent charge relating to the offence.

(4) Where an offender who is bound by the conditions of a probation order made at a time when the offender was directed to be discharged under this section is convicted of an offence, including an offence under section 733.1, the court that made the probation order may, in addition to or in lieu of exercising its authority under subsection 732.2(5), at any time when it may take action under that subsection, revoke the discharge, convict the offender of the offence to which the discharge relates and impose any sentence that could have been imposed if the offender had been convicted at the time of discharge, and no appeal lies from a conviction under this subsection where an appeal was taken from the order directing that the offender be discharged. 1995, c. 22, s. 6; 1997, c. 18, s. 141; 2003, c. 21, s. 17.

1555

Other Available Sentences

The remaining columns of the Offence Grid display other available sentences, including a suspended sentence, a fine alone, and a conditional sentence.

Example 5.5

Find the column of the Offence Grid headed "Conditional Sentence s. 742.1." Section 742.1 of the Code (reproduced below) provides the limitations on this sentence. The circumstances of the offence and the circumstances of the offender establish the limitations of the availability of the conditional sentence.

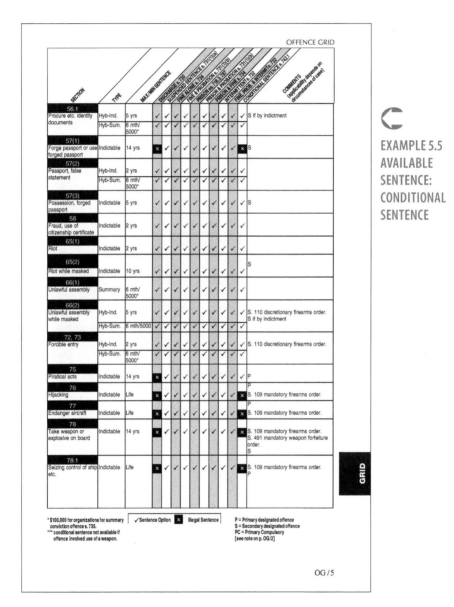

OFFENCE GRID

SECTION	TYPE	MAX/MIN SENTENCE	DISCHARGE s. 730	SUSPENDED SENTENCE & 731(1)(a)	FINE ALONE s. 734	FINE & PROBATION s. 731(1)(b)	PRISON s. 718.3(2)	PRISON & PROBATION s. 731(1)(b)	PRISON & FINE s. 734	INTERMITTENT s. 732	FINE, PROB. & INTERMIT. s. 732	CONDITIONAL SENTENCE s. 742.1	COMMENTS (applicability depends on circumstances of case)
56.1 Procure etc. identity documents	Hyb-Ind.	5 yrs	✓	✓	✓	✓	✓	✓	✓	✓	✓	S if by indictment
	Hyb-Sum.	6 mth/ 5000*	✓	✓	✓	✓	✓	✓	✓	✓	✓	
57(1) Forge passport or use forged passport	Indictable	14 yrs	✗	✓	✓	✓	✓	✓	✓	✓	✗	S
57(2) Passport, false statement	Hyb-Ind.	2 yrs	✓	✓	✓	✓	✓	✓	✓	✓	✓	
	Hyb-Sum.	6 mth/ 5000*	✓	✓	✓	✓	✓	✓	✓	✓	✓	
57(3) Possession, forged passport	Indictable	5 yrs	✓	✓	✓	✓	✓	✓	✓	✓	✓	S
58 Fraud, use of citizenship certificate	Indictable	2 yrs	✓	✓	✓	✓	✓	✓	✓	✓	✓	
65(1) Riot	Indictable	2 yrs	✓	✓	✓	✓	✓	✓	✓	✓	✓	
65(2) Riot while masked	Indictable	10 yrs	✓	✓	✓	✓	✓	✓	✓	✓	✓	S
66(1) Unlawful assembly	Summary	6 mth/ 5000*	✓	✓	✓	✓	✓	✓	✓	✓	✓	
66(2) Unlawful assembly while masked	Hyb-Ind.	5 yrs	✓	✓	✓	✓	✓	✓	✓	✓	✓	S. 110 discretionary firearms order. S if by indictment
	Hyb-Sum.	6 mth/5000	✓	✓	✓	✓	✓	✓	✓	✓	✓	
72, 73 Forcible entry	Hyb-Ind.	2 yrs	✓	✓	✓	✓	✓	✓	✓	✓	✓	S. 110 discretionary firearms order.
	Hyb-Sum.	6 mth/ 5000*	✓	✓	✓	✓	✓	✓	✓	✓	✓	
75 Piratical acts	Indictable	14 yrs	✗	✓	✓	✓	✓	✓	✓	✓	✓	P
76 Hijacking	Indictable	Life	✗	✓	✓	✓	✓	✓	✓	✓	✗	P S. 109 mandatory firearms order.
77 Endanger aircraft	Indictable	Life	✗	✓	✓	✓	✓	✓	✓	✓	✗	P S. 109 mandatory firearms order.
78 Take weapon or explosive on board	Indictable	14 yrs	✗	✓	✓	✓	✓	✓	✓	✓	✗	P S. 109 mandatory firearms order. S. 491 mandatory weapon forfeiture order. S
78.1 Seizing control of ship etc.	Indictable	Life	✗	✓	✓	✓	✓	✓	✓	✓	✗	S. 109 mandatory firearms order. P

* $100,000 for organizations for summary conviction offence s. 735.
*** conditional sentence not available if offence involved use of a weapon.

| ✓Sentence Option | ✗ Illegal Sentence |

P = Primary designated offence
S = Secondary designated offence
PC = Primary Compulsory
[see note on p. OG/2]

OG /5

EXAMPLE 5.5
AVAILABLE
SENTENCE:
CONDITIONAL
SENTENCE

GRID

S. 742.1 MARTIN'S CRIMINAL CODE, 2020

IMPOSING OF CONDITIONAL SENTENCE.

742.1 If a person is convicted of an offence and the court imposes a sentence of imprisonment of less than two years, the court may, for the purpose of supervising the offender's behaviour in the community, order that the offender serve the sentence in the community, subject to the conditions imposed under section 742.3, if

(a) the court is satisfied that the service of the sentence in the community would not endanger the safety of the community and would be consistent with the fundamental purpose and principles of sentencing set out in sections 718 to 718.2;

(b) the offence is not an offence punishable by a minimum term of imprisonment;

(c) the offence is not an offence, prosecuted by way of indictment, for which the maximum term of imprisonment is 14 years or life;

(d) the offence is not a terrorism offence, or a criminal organization offence, prosecuted by way of indictment, for which the maximum term of imprisonment is 10 years or more;

(e) the offence is not an offence, prosecuted by way of indictment, for which the maximum term of imprisonment is 10 years, that

(i) resulted in bodily harm,

(ii) involved the import, export, trafficking or production of drugs, or

(iii) involved the use of a weapon; and

(f) the offence is not an offence, prosecuted by way of indictment, under any of the following provisions:

(i) section 144 (prison breach),

(ii) section 264 (criminal harassment),

(iii) section 271 (sexual assault),

(iv) section 279 (kidnapping),

(v) section 279.02 (trafficking in persons — material benefit),

(vi) section 281 (abduction of person under fourteen),

(vii) section 333.1 (motor vehicle theft),

(viii) paragraph 334(a) (theft over $5000),

(ix) paragraph 348(1)(e) (breaking and entering a place other than a dwelling-house),

(x) section 349 (being unlawfully in a dwelling-house), and

(xi) section 435 (arson for fraudulent purpose). 1995, c. 22, s. 6; 1997, c. 18, s. 107.1; 2007, c. 12, s. 1; 2012, c. 1, s. 34.

CROSS-REFERENCES

Section 718(c) provides that an objective of sentencing is to separate offenders from society "where necessary". It is a principle of sentence under s. 718.2(d) that an offender should not be deprived of liberty if less restrictive sanctions may be appropriate, and under para. (e) that "all available sanctions other than imprisonment that are reasonable in the circumstances should be considered for all offenders, with particular attention to the circumstances of aboriginal offenders."

"Court" is defined in s. 716. Pursuant to s. 742.2, the court, before imposing a conditional sentence under this section, is to consider whether a firearms prohibition must or should be imposed under s. 100. The requirement for such an order is not affected by the fact that the court may also make it an optional condition under s. 742.3(2)(b) that the offender abstain from owning, possessing or carrying a weapon.

The mandatory and optional conditions of a conditional sentence order are set out in s. 742.3. Section 742.3 also sets out the procedure for notifying the offender of the consequences of failure to comply with the conditions and of the possibility of changing the conditions. Pursuant to s. 742 "change" includes deletions and additions. Section 742.3 requires *inter alia* that the offender report to a supervisor while on a conditional sentence. "Supervisor" is defined in s. 742. Section 742.4 allows the supervisor to apply to the court to change the optional conditions of the order.

1592

When determining the available sentences for an offence, the check marks in the Offence Grid are only the first step. It is also necessary to refer to the sentence section. This section will provide the unique circumstances when a sentence is not available for a specific offence or a specific offender.

Other Court Orders

"Comments" is the column on the far right of the Offence Grid. A court may make the listed discretionary orders and must make the listed mandatory orders. Use the section number to find detailed information about the order within the Code. The availability of judicial orders depends on the circumstances of the particular offence.

Example 5.6

Find the "Comments" column for section 88 of the Code, "Possession for purpose dangerous to the public" (reproduced below). Reading across for proceedings by indictment, you will find the first entry under "Comments," which indicates "mandatory firearms order." When there is a finding of guilt, the sentencing judge must impose an order prohibiting the offender from possessing any firearm. The reference is section 109 of the Code.

MARTIN'S CRIMINAL CODE, 2020

SECTION	TYPE	MAX/MIN SENTENCE	DISCHARGE S. 730	SUSPENDED SENTENCE S. 731(1)(a)	FINE ALONE S. 734	FINE & PROBATION S. 731(1)(b)	PRISON & FINE S. 734	PRISON & PROBATION S. 731(1)(b)	INTERMITTENT S. 732	FINE, PROB. & INTERMITTY S. 732	CONDITIONAL SENTENCE S. 742.1	COMMENTS (applicability depends on circumstances of case)
83.23(1)(b) Harbouring terrorist, carried out terrorism offence liable to any other punishment	Indictable	10 yrs	✓	✓	✓	✓	✓	✓	✓	✓	✗	S. 83.26 sentence must be consecutive to any other imposed. P
83.231(2) Terrorist activity, hoax	Hyb-Ind.	5 yrs	✓	✓	✓	✓	✓	✓	✓	✓	✓	S
	Hyb-Sum.	6 mth/ 5000*	✓	✓	✓	✓	✓	✓	✓	✓		
83.231(3) Terrorism, hoax causing bodily harm	Hyb-Ind.	10 yrs	✓	✓	✓	✓	✓	✓	✓	✓	✗	S. 110 discretionary firearms order. S
	Hyb-Sum.	18 mth	✓	✓	✓	✓	✓	✓	✓	✓		
83.231(4) Terrorist hoax, causing death	Indictable	Life	✗	✓	✓	✓	✓	✓	✓	✓	✗	S. 110 discretionary firearms order. S
85 Use of firearm or imitation, commission of offence	Indictable	14 yrs max. Minimums: 1 yr-1st 3 yrs-2nd	✗	✗	✗	✗	**	✓	✗	✗	✗	S. 109 mandatory firearms order. S. 491 mandatory weapon forfeiture order. Sentence must be consecutive to any other imposed. **Not a possible sentence for a second offence because there is a minimum sentence of three years. Higher penalty for second or subsequent offence requires compliance with s. 727.
86 Firearm, careless use or storage, breach of regulations	Hyb-Ind.	Maximums: 2 yrs-1st 5 yrs-2nd	✓	✓	✓	✓	✓	✓	✓	✓	✓	S. 110 discretionary firearms order. S. 491 mandatory weapon forfeiture order. Higher penalty for second or subsequent offence requires compliance with s. 665.
	Hyb-Sum.	6 mth/ 5000*	✓	✓	✓	✓	✓	✓	✓	✓	✓	S (for secondary or subsequent offence if indictable)
87 Firearm, pointing	Hyb-Ind.	5 yrs	✓	✓	✓	✓	✓	✓	✓	✓	✓	S. 110 discretionary firearms order. S. 491 mandatory weapon forfeiture order. S if by indictment
	Hyb-Sum.	6 mth/ 5000*	✓	✓	✓	✓	✓	✓	✓	✓	✓	
88 Possession for purpose dangerous to the public	Hyb-Ind.	10 yrs	✓	✓	✓	✓	✓	✓	✓	✓	*** ✗	S. 109 mandatory firearms order. S. 491 mandatory weapon forfeiture order.
	Hyb-Sum.	6 mth/ 5000*	✓	✓	✓	✓	✓	✓	✓	✓	✓	S. 110 discretionary firearms order. S. 491 mandatory weapon forfeiture order. S if by indictment
89 Weapon at public meeting	Summary	6 mth/ 5000*	✓	✓	✓	✓	✓	✓	✓	✓	✓	S. 110 discretionary firearms order. S. 491 mandatory weapon forfeiture order.

* $100,000 for organizations for summary conviction offence s. 735.
*** conditional sentence not available if offence involved use of a weapon.

✓ Sentence Option   ✗ Illegal Sentence

P = Primary designated offence
S = Secondary designated offence
PC = Primary Compulsory
[see note on p. OG/2]

OG / 8

EXAMPLE 5.6 MANDATORY AND DISCRETIONARY ORDER

Next, find proceedings by summary conviction. Here, the sentencing judge has discretion whether or not to impose a firearms prohibition order. The reference is section 110 of the Code.

For both indictable and summary conviction offences, the "Comments" column indicates "mandatory weapons forfeiture order." This means that when the court finds an accused guilty, the sentencing judge must order the accused to forfeit the weapon used during the offence to the Crown. The weapon will be disposed of as directed by the Attorney General. The reference is section 491 of the Code.

What must a police officer do with a forfeited weapon? According to section 491 of the Code, the officer must contact the agent of the provincial (or territorial) Attorney General. The local Crown attorney is the agent of the Attorney General. As a result, the Crown attorney will provide instructions to the police officer about what to do with the forfeited weapon.

The final entry in the "Comments" column is "S if by indictment." As indicated by the legend at the bottom of the page, "S" means "secondary designated offence," "P" means "primary designated offence," and "PC" means "primary compulsory designated offence." The legend directs the reader to the "note on page OG/2".

Once a person is found guilty or is convicted of specified offences, the court may order the taking of samples of bodily substances for the purpose of forensic DNA analysis. Section 487.04 of the Code defines primary compulsory designated offences, primary designated offences, and secondary designated offences. Section 487.051 of the Code provides the details of the orders.

According to section 3.1 of the Code, judicial orders are effective when they are pronounced. A verbal judicial order has binding authority. For further clarification, an unwritten order has binding authority.

The Offence Grid is an excellent starting point for understanding the offences under the Code. The next step is to examine the relevant sections of the Code, as well as the related Commentary, including the Cross-References, the Synopsis, and the Annotations.

5.6   What sentences are not available for breaking and entering a dwelling-house?

_____

_____

_____

_____

_____

5.7   Are there any mandatory weapons orders for this offence?

_____

_____

_____

_____

5.8   What is the meaning of "P" in the "Comments" column?

_____

_____

_____

_____

CHAPTER 6

Table of Cases

The Table of Cases included in *Martin's Annual Criminal Code* lists alphabetically all of the cases with citations. The next column lists the section numbers associated with the case. The reader will find the case in the commentary of the *Criminal Code* or other statutes, and under the heading Annotations, the reader will find specific information about the case.

Because judgments often address more than one issue, case annotations may cover several issues. Sometimes there will be annotations for the same case under two or more sections of the Code and/or other statutes.

If you are researching an issue and recall the case name, the Table of Cases in Martin's will help you find the annotation.

Example 6.1

Turn to the Table of Cases and find the case name *Martin, R. v.* (reproduced below). There are four different cases under this name on this page. The second one, decided in 1985, lists three section references: "9, 10, (CH)11." The references tell you that the decision in the 1985 case of *R. v. Martin* relates to the interpretation of sections 9 and 10 of the Code and section 11 of the *Canadian Charter of Rights and Freedoms*.

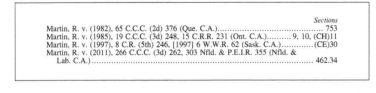

```
                                                                        Sections
Martin, R. v. (1982), 65 C.C.C. (2d) 376 (Que. C.A.)............................................ 753
Martin, R. v. (1985), 19 C.C.C. (3d) 248, 15 C.R.R. 231 (Ont. C.A.)......... 9, 10, (CH)11
Martin, R. v. (1997), 8 C.R. (5th) 246, [1997] 6 W.W.R. 62 (Sask. C.A.)............. (CE)30
Martin, R. v. (2011), 266 C.C.C. (3d) 262, 303 Nfld. & P.E.I.R. 355 (Nfld. &
    Lab. C.A.)................................................................................................ 462.34
```

**EXAMPLE 6.1
SECTION
REFERENCES FOR
A CASE**

Turn to section 9 of the Code. Under the Annotations heading, in the fifth paragraph after the heading Conduct of Other Persons in Court (reproduced below), you will find the reference to *R. v. Martin* (1985), 19 C.C.C. (3d) 248, 15 C.R.R. 231 (Ont. C.A.).

EXAMPLE 6.1
DISCUSSION OF
CASE IN THE
ANNOTATIONS
FOR SECTION 9
OF THE CODE

It was held by the majority in *R. v. Flamand* (1980), 57 C.C.C. (2d) 366 (Que. C.A.), that remarks by an accused to the trial judge that he was not fit to try the case because the judge's son was a police officer and that he (the accused) no longer had confidence in the judge constituted contempt of court being deliberately calculated to bring the trial judge into contempt, lower his authority, cast discredit on the administration of justice and impede its normal course. Mayrand J.A. dissenting would have quashed the conviction on the basis that an expressed lack of confidence in a judge, if a genuinely held belief, even if not justified on a rational basis, does not constitute contempt of court. His Lordship also considered the summary manner in which the proceedings were conducted by the trial judge deprived the accused of an opportunity to present a full and complete defence. On further appeal [1982] 1 S.C.R. 337, 65 C.C.C. (2d) 192*n*, 42 N.R. 87 (7:0), the dissenting judgment of Mayrand J.A. was approved and the conviction quashed.

Abusive language by an accused attributing gross insensitivity to the trial judge could be viewed as calculated to lower his authority and thus capable of constituting contempt of court: *R. v. Martin* (1985), 19 C.C.C. (3d) 248, 15 C.R.R. 231 (Ont. C.A.).

Next turn to section 10 of the Code. Then turn to section 11 of the Charter. Under the Annotations heading for these sections (reproduced below), you will again find references to the 1985 case of *R. v. Martin*.

EXAMPLE 6.1
DISCUSSION OF
CASE IN THE
ANNOTATIONS FOR
SECTION 10 OF THE
CODE

Proceedings for contempt of court arising out of abusive remarks by the accused to the trial judge after he convicted her, having made adverse findings of credibility, ought not to have been tried by that same judge. In the circumstances, the accused could have a reasonable apprehension of bias and her rights under s. 11(*d*) of the Charter were infringed: *R. v. Martin* (1985), 19 C.C.C. (3d) 248 (Ont. C.A.).

EXAMPLE 6.1
DISCUSSION OF
CASE IN THE
ANNOTATIONS
FOR SECTION 11
OF THE CHARTER

Trial by independent tribunal [s. 11(*d*)] – Generally speaking, where the alleged contemptuous language or actions are insulting and insolent it is preferable that any contempt proceedings be taken before a judge other than the judge to whom the remarks were addressed: *R. v. Martin* (1985), 19 C.C.C. (3d) 248 (Ont. C.A.).

Judicial independence involves both individual and institutional relationships. The individual independence of a judge is reflected in such matters as security of tenure, and the institutional independence of the court or tribunal over which he presides is reflected in its institutional or administrative relationship to the executive and legislative branches of government. The test for independence for the purposes of s. 11(*d*) is whether the tribunal may reasonably be perceived as independent. Both independence and impartiality are fundamental not only to the capacity to do justice in a particular case but also to individual and public confidence in the administration of justice. It is important that a tribunal should be perceived as independent and that the test for independence should include that perception. The perception must however be a perception of whether the tribunal enjoys the essential objective conditions or guarantees of judicial independence, not a perception of how it will in fact act, regardless of whether it enjoys such conditions or guarantees. The standard of judicial independence must necessarily be a standard that reflects what is common to, or at the heart of, various approaches to the essential conditions of judicial independence in Canada and need not be a standard of uniform provisions such as the standard embodied in the *Constitution Act, 1867* for superior court judges: *R. v. Valente*, [1985] 2 S.C.R. 673, 23 C.C.C. (3d) 193.

In the Table of Cases, you may find more than one case under the same name or initials, for example, *R. v. Martin*. How will you know which case is the one you need to read about for your research?

Example 6.2

You want to search for information about the *Archer* case. You think the case answered a question about weapons, and you believe that the court decided the case in the early 1980s. When you search for *Archer* in the Table of Cases (reproduced below), you find five cases by that name.

A quick examination narrows your search to two cases decided in the early 1980s. Notice that one case lists sections 84 and 91 of the Code, contained in Part III / Firearms and Other Weapons. You have narrowed your search further. Using the citation, you can locate the correct reference in the Annotations.

Different levels of court may examine the same case. The trial judge provides the first decision at the lowest court. Often the trial judge provides the most detailed discussion of the facts of the case. When a trial judge provides written reasons for a judgment, he or she relies on all of the facts presented at the trial to reach a conclusion. The trial judge determines the credibility of witnesses and the admissibility of evidence. Therefore, the written judgment of the trial judge includes all of the facts required to decide the outcome of the case.

By contrast, an appeal occurs only if a dissatisfied party believes there was an error at a lower court. Thus, a court of appeal is restricted to the grounds of appeal raised by a dissatisfied party. As a result, a court of appeal includes only the facts necessary to decide the appeal and is limited to the facts required to answer the question posed by legal counsel at the appeal. Thus, reading the appeal judgment may not provide a complete picture of the case. Therefore, it is beneficial to read lower court judgments.

Judges at appellate courts have the ability to confirm or overrule a lower court decision. However, the name of a case does not change during an appeal. The court of appeal may review a lower court decision regarding a specific issue. However, if a case has multiple legal issues, the lower court's decision and reasons may continue to provide clarity about certain issues in the case.

Arabia, R. v. (2008), 235 C.C.C. (3d) 354, 240 O.A.C. 104 (C.A.).............................. 650
Aranda, R. v. (1992), 69 C.C.C. (3d) 420, 6 O.R. (3d) 776 (Gen. Div.)..................... 187
Arason, R. v. (1992), 78 C.C.C. (3d) 1, 37 W.A.C. 20 (B.C.C.A.)........................... (CD)5
Araujo, R. v., [2000] 2 S.C.R. 992, 149 C.C.C. (3d) 449 .... 185, 186, 487, 676, (CH)8
Aravena, R. v. (2015), 323 C.C.C. (3d) 54, 20 C.R. (7th) 131 (Ont. C.A.), leave
  to appeal to S.C.C. refused 2016 CarswellOnt 5400, leave to appeal to S.C.C.
  refused 2016 CarswellOnt 5404, leave to appeal to S.C.C. refused 2016
  CarswellOnt 5410 17
Arcand, R. v. (2010), 264 C.C.C. (3d) 134, 83 C.R. (6th) 199 (Alta. C.A.) 718.2
Archer, R. v. (1972), 26 C.R.N.S. 225 (Ont. C.A.).. 650
Archer, R. v. (1981), 59 C.C.C. (2d) 384, 21 C.R. (3d) 352 (Ont. C.A.).................. 522
Archer, R. v. (1983), 6 C.C.C. (3d) 129 (Ont. C.A.)... 84, 91
Archer, R. v. (1989), 47 C.C.C. (3d) 567, 65 Alta. L.R. (2d) 183 (C.A.) .... (CE)37.1
Archer, R. v. (2005), 193 C.C.C. (3d) 376, 193 O.A.C. 344 (C.A.) 753
Arcuri, R. v., [2001] 2 S.C.R. 828, 157 C.C.C. (3d) 21.................................... 541, 548
Argentina (Republic) v. Mellion, [1987] 1 S.C.R. 536, 33 C.C.C. (3d) 334 .... (CH)7
Arkell, R. v., [1990] 2 S.C.R. 695, 59 C.C.C. (3d) 65 .... 31, (CH)7

**EXAMPLE 6.2
DIFFERENT CASES
LISTED UNDER
THE SAME NAME**

EXERCISES

6.1   Search for *Phillips v. Nova Scotia (Commission of Inquiry into the Westray Mine Tragedy)* in the Table of Cases. Which section of which statute should you refer to for information about this case?

_____

_____

_____

_____

_____

6.2   You are researching whether a dog can be a weapon. Your professor mentioned the *McLeod* case. You search for *McLeod* in the Table of Cases and discover that there are several. How can you identify the case you want?

_____

_____

_____

_____

_____

6.3   What section of the Code relates to assault with a weapon?

_____

_____

_____

_____

_____

6.4   Which of the *McLeod* cases determines whether a dog is a weapon under the Code?

_____

_____

_____

_____

_____

CHAPTER 7

Criminal Code Concordance

The *Criminal Code* Concordance cross-references the parts and sections of the current Code with the parts and sections of the previous Code. More particularly, the current *Martin's Annual Criminal Code* compares *Criminal Code* R.S.C. 1985, c. C-46 with the previous revision, R.S.C. 1970, c. C-34. The Concordance is located after the Table of Contents and immediately following the Preface.

The Concordance has two columns. The left-hand column lists the previous parts and sections of the 1970 revision. The right-hand column lists the current parts and sections of the 1985 revision and all subsequent amendments.

Amendments to the Code

The Canadian Parliament passed the first Code in 1892, and there have been several revisions since then. Why do the part and section numbers change?

Canada's Parliament makes changes to federal statutes by removing, adding, or modifying sections. Specifically, Parliament changes the Code to be responsive to Canadian society.

First, Parliament repeals sections of legislation. Specifically, when Parliament repeals a section of a statute, it removes that section. Second, Parliament amends sections of legislation. Specifically, it amends legislation by adding a section to a statute. Parliament also amends legislation by revising a section of a statute.

For example, in 2018, Parliament amended the impaired operation and summary conviction sentencing sections of the Code. First, Parliament repealed section 255. Second, Parliament added section 320.19. Third, Parliament revised section 787.

Revision of a Statute

Parliament may revise a statute by changing section numbers and renumbering parts of the statute. The most recent revision of the Code occurred during the creation of the *Revised Statutes of Canada* in 1985.

Researching Judicial Decisions

Judicial decisions or judgments often interpret a word or phrase within a section of a statute. Judges write court decisions at a specific date. Therefore, decisions do not reflect changes to part or section numbers that happen after the date of the decision. Section numbers in judgments given before the last Code revision will refer to the section number of an earlier version of the Code. As a result, changes to section numbers can present a challenge for researchers. The Concordance matches the old section number and the new section number for the same provision.

Consider section 265 of the Code, which defines the substantive offence of assault. Assault was deemed a criminal offence in *Criminal Code* 1892, 55-56 Vict., c. 29. Therefore, many judgments are referred to in the Annotations following section 265 of the Code. Some decisions predate the 1985 revision to the Code. Older judgments refer to assault under section 301 of the Code because it is the previous section number for the offence of assault under R.S.C. 1970, c. C-34.

Example 7.1

In the right-hand column for R.S.C. 1985, c. C-46, find the current section 322 of the Code, Theft (reproduced below). It is the second provision in Part IX. Look across to the left-hand column. The previous number for the section offence of theft was section 283 of Part VII of R.S.C. 1970, c. C-34.

Thus, the Concordance tells you that the section for the offence of theft was section 283 of the Code from 1970 to 1985. After 1985, it was renumbered as section 322 of the Code.

<table>
<tr><td rowspan="5">⮕

**EXAMPLE 7.1
RENUMBERING OF
SECTIONS**</td><td>R.S.C. 1970, c. C-34</td><td>R.S.C. 1985, c. C-46</td></tr>
<tr><td>Part VII</td><td>Part IX</td></tr>
<tr><td>282</td><td>321</td></tr>
<tr><td>283</td><td>322</td></tr>
<tr><td>284</td><td>323</td></tr>
</table>

Example 7.2

In the right-hand column for R.S.C. 1985, c. C-46, find the current subsection 271(2) (reproduced below). Look across to the left-hand column. The corresponding reference is to subsection 246.1(2) of R.S.C. 1970, c. C-34.

The Concordance will also inform you if a section has been repealed. As in Example 7.1, the Concordance shows that the Code was revised in 1985. Subsection 246.1(2) of the Code was renumbered as subsection 271(2). Additionally, we find the following information: "[rep. R.S.C. 1985, c. 19 (3rd Supp.), s. 10]."

The Concordance tells us that subsection 271(2) of the Code was repealed by section 10 of the *Revised Statutes of Canada*, 1985, chapter 19, third supplement. Thus, the subsection is no longer in force and is not included in the current version of the Code.

During revision of the Code, sections are removed. Thus, the reader will no longer see those sections, and the Code is not renumbered. Additionally, those sections no longer have the force of law. In the right-hand column of the Concordance, you will find the word "repealed."

R.S.C. 1970, c. C-34	R.S.C. 1985, c. C-46
—	270.03 [en. 2015, c. 34, s. 2]
—	270.1 [en. 2002, c. 13, s. 11]
246.1	271
246.1(2)	271(2) [rep. R.S.C. 1985, c. 19 (3rd Supp.), s. 10]
246.2	272
246.3	273

C

EXAMPLE 7.2
REPEALED
PROVISION

Example 7.3

In the left-hand column for R.S.C. 1970, c. C-34, find the previous section 13 (reproduced below). Look across to the right-hand column. The corresponding reference is "repealed."

The Concordance indicates that previous section 13 of R.S.C. 1970, c. C-34 was repealed by R.S.C. 1985, c. C-46. Thus, that provision is not included in the current version of the Code. The current section 13 is a different provision.

EXAMPLE 7.3
REPEALED
PROVISION

R.S.C. 1970, c. C-34	R.S.C. 1985, c. C-46
7(1)(a)	8(1)(b)
7(1)(b)	8(1)(a)
8	9
9	10
10	11
11	12
12	13
13	repealed
14-33	14-33

The revision of the Code in 1985 and further amendments after that date created new parts. The revision also renumbered other parts and sections.

Example 7.4

Review the entry in the R.S.C. 1985, c. C-46 column, "Part XXI.1 [en. 2002, c. 13, s. 71]." A new part (Part XXI.1) was enacted in an amendment in 2002, numbered as section 71 in chapter 13 of the amending Act.

EXAMPLE 7.4
ENACTMENT OF
A NEW PART

R.S.C. 1970, c. C-34	R.S.C. 1985, c. C-46
—	695(2) [rep. 1999, c. 3, s. 27]
624	696
—	Part XXI.1 [en. 2002, c. 13, s. 71]
625	697

Example 7.5

A renumbering of parts is on the next page of the Concordance (reproduced below). Part XXII in R.S.C. 1970, c. C-34 became Part XXV in R.S.C. 1985, c. C-46. Part XXIII became Part XXVI, and Part XXIV became Part XXVII.

R.S.C. 1970, c. C-34	R.S.C. 1985, c. C-46
695	760
695.1	761
Part XXII	Part XXV
696	762
697	763
698	764
699	765
700	766
701	767
701.1	767.1
702	768
703	769
704	770
705	771
706	772
707	773
Part XXIII	Part XXVI
708	774
—	774.1 [en. 2002, c. 13, s. 77]
709	775
710	776
711	777
712	778
713	779
714	780
715	781
716	782
717	783
718	repealed
719	784
Part XXIV	Part XXVII
720	785
—	785 "sentence" (*d*) [en. 1997, c. 19, s. 76]

EXAMPLE 7.5
RENUMBERING
OF PARTS

7.1   In the Concordance, review the current section 487 of the Code, Information for Search Warrant. What was the section number before the 1985 *Revised Statutes of Canada* were published?

_____

_____

_____

_____

_____

7.2   Paragraph 487(1) (c.1) of the Code permits the search of "any offence-related property." Did the paragraph exist in 1985 when the last *Revised Statutes of Canada* were published?

_____

_____

_____

_____

_____

Historical Offences: "Cold Cases"

The Concordance assists with historical offences or "cold cases." Historical offences are criminal offences that occurred years ago. Often provisions of the Code change between the time of the criminal offence and the current investigation.

Cold cases are new or revived investigations. A case is revived because advanced investigative techniques or additional information creates the opportunity for law enforcement professionals to obtain more evidence. Most often, these cases involve sexual offences and murder.

There is a limitation period of 12 months from the time of the allegation for a summary conviction offence until prosecution. However, proceedings for many offences under the Code and the *Controlled Drugs and Substances Act* may start at any time. They include both indictable and hybrid offences. Hybrid offences are also known as dual procedure offences. Hybrid offences may commence by either a summary conviction procedure or an indictable procedure. Therefore, allegations of criminal conduct that took place more than 30 years ago can become the source of an investigation leading to current charges.

The current Code includes several sexual assault provisions. Prior to 1983, an act of sexual intercourse without consent was rape, contrary to section 143 of the Code. However, during the early 1980s, there was a shift in thinking in Canadian criminal law about sexual assault. The change in attitude led to the amalgamation of the sexual offences against adult complainants.

First, to convict the accused, you must prove the elements of the offence that existed at the time of the offence. Second, you must find the Code applicable at that time. Third, you must find the correct provision. Fourth, in order to correctly draft the Information (Form 2), you must use the wording of the charge that existed at the time of the offence. Thus, you must examine the wording carefully.

Start at the library to find the correct provision. Find three annotated annual Codes, such as Martin's, which has been published annually since 1955. The three editions required are one published in the year in which the offence allegedly occurred, one published in the year prior to the offence, and one published in the year following the offence.

Review all three editions. You are searching for any amendments that have been passed around the time of the alleged criminal offence. If there are amendments, you must examine the dates to determine which version of the provision applied on the date of the alleged criminal offence.

What section will you review? The Concordance provides you with an answer. If you are still unable to locate the correct section, use the index in the edition that you are searching to find the subject, for example, sexual assault.

EXERCISES

7.3   A rape case from January 1973 is reinvestigated, and a DNA match is discovered. Can the current sexual assault provisions be used in the Information?

_____

_____

_____

_____

_____

Legislative History

Further details about legislative changes are available in each section of the Code. At the end of each section, there is a reference to one or more enactments. The references are the legislative history for that particular section.

Martin's includes a list of all of the legislative references. The first ten pages of the Code include every amending enactment made to the Code since R.S.C. 1985, c. C-46. Thus, you can determine the date on which a section came into force.

Example 7.6

Review the list of amendments on page 4 (reproduced below). Specifically, the entry starts with "Amended 1997, c. 18, ss. 1 to 115; s. 107.1 and 139.1 in force May 2, 1997." Match the information with the reference following subsection 786(2) of the Code in Martin's. The change in criminal procedure expressed in subsection 786(2) of the Code (section 110 of the amending statute) became effective on May 2, 1997.

All of the related statutes in Martin's, the *Canada Evidence Act*, the *Controlled Drugs and Substances Act*, the *Crimes Against Humanity and War Crimes Act*, S.C. 2000, c. 24, and the *Youth Criminal Justice Act*, also include the legislative history. All amendments for the statute are listed at the beginning. Martin's provides additional legislative history details at the end of each amended section.

Example 7.7

Review section 177 of the Code, Application of Part / Limitation, from the 2020 edition of Martin's (reproduced below). At the end of the section, there are two legislative references. The first is "R.S., c. C-34, 173," which is a duplication of the information in the Concordance. The first reference was also included in the 1996 and 2010 editions of Martin's.

The second reference is "2018, c. 29, s. 14." Review section 177 of the Code in the 2020 edition of Martin's (reproduced below). Compare section 177 of the Code with the 2010 edition. In the 2020 edition, the words "the proof of which lies on him" have been removed.

Amended 1995, c. 39, ss. 138 to 157, 163, 164, 188(*a*) and (*b*), 189(*e*) and 190; that part of s. 139 which replaces s. 85 and ss. 141 to 150 brought into force January 1, 1996, by SI/96-2, *Can. Gaz., Part II*, January 10, 1996; ss. 138, 139 (except to the extent that it replaces ss. 85 and 97 of the *Criminal Code*), 140, 151 to 157, 163, 164, 188(*a*) and (*b*), 189(*e*), 190 brought into force December 1, 1998 by SI/98-93, *Can. Gaz., Part II*, September 30, 1998 (in force date amended by SI/98-95, *Can. Gaz., Part II*, September 30, 1998); that part of s. 139 which replaces s. 97 to come into force by order of the Governor in Council; however, repealed before coming into force

Amended 1995, c. 42, ss. 73 to 76, 86 and 87; brought into force January 24, 1996 by SI/96-10, *Can. Gaz., Part II*, February 7, 1996 (see ss. 86 and 87)

Amended 1996, c. 7, s. 38; brought into force July 31, 1996 by SI/96-57, Can. Gaz., Part II, July 10, 1996

Amended 1996, c. 8, s. 32(1)(*d*); brought into force July 12, 1996 by SI/96-69, *Can. Gaz., Part II*, July 24, 1996

Amended 1996, c. 16, s. 60(1)(*d*); brought into force July 12, 1996 by SI/96-67, *Can. Gaz., Part II*, July 24, 1996

Amended 1996, c. 19, ss. 65 to 76 and 93.3; ss. 65 to 76 brought into force May 14, 1997 by SI/97-47, *Can. Gaz., Part II*, May 14, 1997; s. 93.3 in force December 1, 1998 as provided by that section

Amended 1996, c. 31, ss. 67 to 72; brought into force January 31, 1997 by SI/97-21, *Can. Gaz., Part II*, February 5, 1997

Amended 1996, c. 34, ss. 1 and 2(2); s. 2(2) in force January 1, 1997; s. 1 to come into force by order of the Governor in Council (repealed before coming into force 2008, c. 20, s. 3)

Amended 1997, c. 16, s. 2; brought into force May 26, 1997 by SI/97-66, *Can. Gaz., Part II*

Amended 1997, c. 17, ss. 1 to 10; brought into force August 1, 1997 by SI/97-84, *Can. Gaz., Part II*, July 23, 1997

Amended 1997, c. 18, ss. 1 to 115; ss. 107.1 and 139.1 in force May 2, 1997 by SI/97-60, *Can. Gaz., Part II*, May 14, 1997; ss. 1, 23, 27 to 39, 99, 100, 109 and 140 in force May 14, 1997 by SI/97-62, *Can. Gaz., Part II*, May 28, 1997; ss. 2 to 22, 24 to 26, 40 to 98, 101 to 105, 108, 110 to 115 and 141 in force June 16, 1997 by SI/97-68, *Can. Gaz., Part II*, June 25, 1997; ss. 106 and 107 to come into force by order of the Governor in Council (repealed before coming into force 2008, c. 20, s. 3)

Amended 1997, c. 23, ss. 1 to 20 and 26; ss. 1 to 20 in force May 2, 1997 by SI/97-61, *Can. Gaz., Part II*, May 14, 1997; s. 26 brought into force December 1, 1998

Amended 1997, c. 30; brought into force May 12, 1997 by SI/97-63, *Can. Gaz., Part II*, May 28, 1997

Amended 1997, c. 39, ss. 1 to 3; in force December 18, 1997

Amended 1998, c. 7, ss. 2, 3; brought into force May 1, 2000 by SI/2000-25, *Can. Gaz., Part II*, April 26, 2000

Amended 1998, c. 9, ss. 2 to 8; brought into force June 30, 1998 by SI/98-79, *Can. Gaz., Part II*, June 24, 1998

Amended 1998, c. 30, ss. 14(*d*) and 16 (and see ss. 10 and 11); brought into force April 19, 1999 by SI/99-37, *Can. Gaz., Part II*, April 28, 1999

Amended 1998, c. 34, ss. 8, 9 and 11; ss. 8 and 9 brought into force February 14, 1999 by SI/99-13, *Can. Gaz., Part II*, March 3, 1999; s. 11 in force September 1, 1999 (as provided by s. 11)

Amended 1998, c. 35, ss. 119 to 121; brought into force September 1, 1999 by SI/99-75, *Can. Gaz., Part II*, July 21, 1999

Amended 1998, c. 37, ss. 15 to 24; brought into force June 30, 2000 by SI/2000-60, *Can. Gaz., Part II*, July 19, 2000

⊂

EXAMPLE 7.6 LEGISLATIVE HISTORY: LIST OF AMENDMENTS

TRESPASSING AT NIGHT.

177. Every person who, without lawful excuse, loiters or prowls at night on the property of another person near a dwelling-house situated on that property is guilty of an offence punishable on summary conviction. R.S., c. C-34, s. 173; 2018, c. 29, s. 14.

⊂

EXAMPLE 7.7 LEGISLATIVE HISTORY: MARTIN'S 2020 EDITION

7.4 Can you determine on what date conduct generally described as "motor vehicle theft" became a specifically defined substantive criminal offence?

_____

_____

_____

_____

_____

7.5 Review "Amended 2002, c. 13" on the list of amendments preceding the Code. Different portions of the amending Act, numbered chapter 13, came into force on different dates. On what date did section 11 of the amending Act come into force?

_____

_____

_____

_____

_____

CHAPTER 8

Commentary: Cross-References, Synopsis, and Annotations

Introduction

The commentary follows most sections of *Martin's Annual Criminal Code* and includes three sections: Cross-References, Synopsis, and Annotations.

Leading criminal lawyers write the commentary. It aids you in understanding a section of the *Criminal Code* and describes how courts have interpreted and applied it. The commentary distinguishes Martin's from the Code published by the Government of Canada.

Cross-References

The Cross-References indicate additional information about the section you are reading. When reviewing a section, the Cross-References identify related sections of the Code and other statutes. For example, following section 92 of the Code, Possession of Firearm Knowing Its Possession Is Unauthorized, the Cross-References list sections of the *Firearms Act*, S.C. 1995, c. 39. They also help readers review these sections and provide definitions for terms such as "firearm" and "possession."

The Cross-References also identify sections of the *Canadian Charter of Rights and Freedoms* and the *Interpretation Act*, R.S.C. 1985, c. I-21.

Example 8.1

Review section 12 of the Code, Offence Punishable Under More than One Act (reproduced below). The section prohibits punishing a person under more than one statute for the same offence. For example, a person breaks into a doctor's office and steals morphine tablets. Because of a silent alarm, the police are able to arrest the person leaving the building. The police may charge the person with committing breaking and entering under section 348 and committing theft under section 334 of the Code. The police may also charge the person with possession of a substance included in Schedule I, contrary to section 4 of the *Controlled Drugs and Substances Act*.

The Cross-References following section 12 of the Code identify a number of sections within the Code and in the Charter that will help determine whether this section applies in a particular case. The Cross-References direct readers to sources for further research and may save them considerable time during their research.

The Cross-References identify definitions in the Code (including section 2), definitions in other statutes, and definitions from judicial decisions.

EXAMPLE 8.1
RELATED
SECTIONS AND
OTHER SOURCES

> **OFFENCE PUNISHABLE UNDER MORE THAN ONE ACT.**
> 12. Where an act or omission is an offence under more than one Act of Parliament, whether punishable by indictment or on summary conviction, a person who does the act or makes the omission is, unless a contrary intention appears, subject to proceedings under any of those Acts, but is not liable to be punished more than once for the same offence. R.S., c. C-34, s. 11.
>
> CROSS-REFERENCES
> As to an *autrefois* plea, see ss. 7(6), 607 to 610 of the Code and s. 11(*h*) of the *Charter of Rights and Freedoms*. As to the abuse of process generally, see notes following s. 579. As to the common law rule precluding multiple convictions for same *delict*, the "*Kienapple*" rule and common law principles of *res judicata* and issue estoppel, see notes following s. 613.

Example 8.2

Review the Cross-References under section 119 of the Code, Bribery of Judicial Officers, Etc. / Consent of Attorney General (reproduced below).

The Cross-References direct readers to definitions of words used in section 119 of the Code, including "office" and "corruptly." For example, section 118 of the Code defines "office," and the court in *R. v. Brown* (1956), 116 C.C.C. 287 (Ont. C.A.), defined "corruptly."

The Cross-References have a wealth of information. They may provide information for classroom discussions. They will also assist when researching criminal law. Furthermore, if the Cross-References direct readers to another statute included in Martin's, the related statute is immediately available. Readers may also find relevant legislation in *Martin's Related Criminal Statutes*.

Corruption and Disobedience

BRIBERY OF JUDICIAL OFFICERS, ETC. / Consent of Attorney General.

119. (1) Every one is guilty of an indictable offence and liable to imprisonment for a term not exceeding fourteen years who

    (*a*) being the holder of a judicial office, or being a member of Parliament or of the legislature of a province, directly or in-directly, corruptly accepts, obtains, agrees to accept or attempts to obtain, for themselves or another person, any money, valuable consideration, office, place or employment in respect of anything done or omitted or to be done or omitted by them in their official capacity, or

    (*b*) directly or indirectly, corruptly gives or offers to a person mentioned in paragraph (*a*), or to anyone for the benefit of that person, any money, valuable consideration, office, place or employment in respect of anything done or omitted or to be done or omitted by that person in their official capacity.

(2) No proceedings against a person who holds a judicial office shall be instituted under this section without the consent in writing of the Attorney General of Canada. R.S., c. C-34, s. 108; 2007, c. 13, s. 3.

CROSS-REFERENCES
The term "office" is defined in s. 118. The term "corruptly" is not defined in this Part but has been considered by the courts in relation to the secret commission offence in s. 426 where it was held not to mean wickedly or dishonestly but to refer to an act done *mala fides*, designed wholly or partially for the purpose of bringing about the effect forbidden by the section: *R. v. Brown* (1956), 116 C.C.C. 287 (Ont. C.A.).

    This offence may be the basis for an application for an authorization to intercept private communications by reason of s. 183. Conviction for this offence may, in some circumstances, result in loss of the office by virtue of s. 748(1) and other disabilities as prescribed by s. 748(2).

    Where the accused is the holder of a judicial office, the consent in writing of the Attorney General of Canada is required (subsec. (2)) and the offence may only be tried by a superior court of criminal jurisdiction (defined in s. 2) by virtue of ss. 468 and 469. [Note, attempt and conspiracy to commit the offence by the holder of a judicial office would not fall within the exclusive jurisdiction of the superior court.] It would also seem that, by virtue of s. 522, only a judge of a superior court can release on bail in such circumstances.

    In all other cases, the accused has an election as to mode of trial under s. 536(2) and release pending trial is dealt with under s. 515.

**EXAMPLE 8.2
RELATED SECTION
AND OTHER
SOURCES**

EXERCISES

8.1   Review the Cross-References for section 343 of the Code, Robbery. Where is the definition of "offensive weapon"? Where is the definition of "assault"? Where is the punishment set out?

_____

_____

_____

_____

_____

8.2   Review the Cross-References for section 175 of the Code, Causing Disturbance, Indecent Exhibition, Loitering, Etc. / Evidence of Peace Officer. What are two of the related offences?

_____

_____

_____

_____

_____

Synopsis

The Synopsis explains the legislative language of the statute as the legal language and structure of a section may be confusing to readers. Thus, the Synopsis helps readers understand the statute.

The Synopsis may also include further explanation and analysis. In particular, the Synopsis for section 265 of the Code, Assault, applies to all forms of assault. As a result, there is no Synopsis following section 271 of the Code, Sexual Assault. However, the Cross-References under section 271 of the Code refer readers to the definition of assault in section 265 of the Code.

Example 8.3

Review section 348 of the Code, Breaking and Entering with Intent, Committing Offence or Breaking Out / Presumptions / Definition of *Place* (reproduced below). The section is complex, but the Synopsis for section 348 of the Code (reproduced below) is concise and effectively explains the meaning of the section.

Breaking and Entering

BREAKING AND ENTERING WITH INTENT, COMMITTING OFFENCE OR BREAKING OUT / Presumptions / Definition of "place".

348. (1) Every one who
  (*a*) breaks and enters a place with intent to commit an indictable offence therein,
  (*b*) breaks and enters a place and commits an indictable offence therein, or
  (*c*) breaks out of a place after
    (i) committing an indictable offence therein, or
    (ii) entering the place with intent to commit an indictable offence therein,
is guilty
  (*d*) if the offence is committed in relation to a dwelling-house, of an indictable offence and liable to imprisonment for life, and
  (*e*) if the offence is committed in relation to a place other than a dwelling-house, of an indictable offence and liable to imprisonment for a term not exceeding ten years or of an offence punishable on summary conviction.

(2) For the purposes of proceedings under this section, evidence that an accused
  (*a*) broke and entered a place or attempted to break and enter a place is, in the absence of evidence to the contrary, proof that he broke and entered the place or attempted to do so, as the case may be, with intent to commit an indictable offence therein; or
  (*b*) broke out of a place is, in the absence of any evidence to the contrary, proof that he broke out after
    (i) committing an indictable offence therein, or
    (ii) entering with intent to commit an indictable offence therein.

(3) For the purposes of this section and section 351, "place" means
  (*a*) a dwelling-house;
  (*b*) a building or structure or any part thereof, other than a dwelling-house;
  (*c*) a railway vehicle, a vessel, an aircraft or a trailer; or
  (*d*) a pen or an enclosure in which fur-bearing animals are kept in captivity for breeding or commercial purposes. R.S., c. C-34, s. 306; 1972, c. 13, s. 24; R.S.C. 1985, c. 27 (1st Supp.), s. 47; 1997, c. 18, s. 20.

**EXAMPLE 8.3
A COMPLEX
SECTION OF THE
CODE**

SYNOPSIS
This section describes the offence of breaking and entering. The offence is committed by anyone: (a) who breaks and enters a place *with intent to commit an indictable offence* therein; (b) who breaks and enters a place and actually commits an indictable offence; or (c) breaks out of a place after committing an indictable offence, or after having entered intending to commit an indictable offence. The offence is indictable, with a maximum punishment of life imprisonment if the place is a dwelling house. For a non-dwelling-house the offence is a hybrid, the maximum punishment being 10 years by indictment and 6 months if the Crown elects to proceed summarily. The meaning of "place", for the purpose of this section, is defined by subsec. (3). Subsection (2) creates two presumptions. Where a person breaks and enters a place or attempts to do so, those acts are proof, in the absence of evidence to the contrary, that the person had the intent to commit an indictable offence therein. Similarly, where a person breaks out of a place, that act is proof that he committed, or entered with intent to commit, an indictable offence therein.

EXAMPLE 8.3
A CONCISE
EXPLANATION OF
THE SECTION

EXERCISES

8.3   Read section 354 of the Code, Possession of Property Obtained by Crime / Obliterated Vehicle Identification Number / Definition of *Vehicle Identification Number* / Exception. Write your own synopsis. Compare it to the Synopsis provided in Martin's. Did you interpret the wording in a similar way? Did reading the Martin's Synopsis improve your understanding of the section? Would it have been easier to understand the section if you had read Martin's Synopsis first?

_____

_____

_____

_____

8.4   Select and read any section of the Code. Read the Synopsis and the Cross-References. Was it beneficial to have read the Synopsis before the Cross-References? Choose and read another section. Read the Cross-References before the Synopsis. Is there an order that works better for you?

_____

_____

_____

_____

Annotations

The Annotations are brief summaries of judicial decisions. Judicial decisions or judgments often interpret a word or phrase within a section of a statute. The Annotations also quote or explain the comments of the court.

The Annotations are an excellent way to start your research. Martin's Annotations are sufficient for a basic understanding of the law. However, if you require deeper analysis, the case citation will assist you to access the full text of the judgment.

Example 8.4

Review section 177 of the Code, Trespassing at Night. What is the meaning of "prowls at night"? The Cross-References to section 177 of the Code indicate that section 2 of the Code defines "night." However, what is the definition of "prowls"? Review the Annotations (reproduced below).

In *R. v. Cloutier* (1991), 66 C.C.C. (3d) 149, the Quebec Court of Appeal held that prowling "includes a notion of evil" and that a prowler has a purpose. A British Columbia lower court decision in *R. v. Willis* (1987), 37 C.C.C. (3d) 184 (B.C. Co. Ct.), interpreted "prowl" as "to traverse stealthily," in the sense of "furtively, secretly, clandestinely, or moving by imperceptible degrees."

EXAMPLE 8.4
MEANING OF
"PROWLS"

> ANNOTATIONS
> This section creates two offences of prowling and loitering. The essence of loitering is the conduct of someone who is wandering about apparently without precise destination and is conduct which essentially has nothing reprehensible about it, if it does not take place on private property where the loiterer has no business. Prowling, on the other hand, involves some notion of evil. The prowler does not act without a purpose: *R. v. Cloutier* (1991), 66 C.C.C. (3d) 149 (Que. C.A.).
> "Prowls" means to traverse stealthily in the sense of furtively, secretly, clandestinely or moving by imperceptible degrees. The Crown need not prove that the accused was looking for an opportunity to carry out an unlawful purpose. It is not a lawful excuse within the meaning of this section that the accused was trying to conceal himself following commission of a criminal offence: *R. v. Willis* (1987), 37 C.C.C. (3d) 184 (B.C. Co. Ct.).

EXERCISES

8.5 An accused gets into a loud swearing match with a friend in a secluded laneway. Will there be a conviction under section 175 of the Code, Causing Disturbance, Indecent Exhibition, Loitering, etc.? What if there is a passerby?

_____

_____

_____

_____

_____

8.6 Paragraph (d) of section 343 of the Code, Robbery, states that a person commits robbery who "steals … while armed with an offensive weapon or imitation thereof." During a criminal investigation, you discover that an accused imitated having a gun by holding up his hand with his first finger pointing forward and thumb up. Could a court find the person guilty under paragraph 343(d) of the Code?

_____

_____

_____

_____

_____

Stare Decisis

Stare decisis is Latin for "let the decision stand." The principle of *stare decisis* promotes consistency and predictability in the law. Readers must know both the level and the location of the court to determine the precedence of a decision.

Level of Court

The principle dictates that lower courts must follow the rulings of higher courts. The Supreme Court of Canada (SCC) is the ultimate court of appeal for all Canadian courts. As a result, all Canadian courts must follow the decisions of the SCC.

Location of Court

Another factor to consider is the location of the court. The location of the court will determine whether a decision is binding, and a lower court must follow a binding decision. Canada is a confederation of provinces; thus, each province has its own hierarchy of courts. For example, a decision of the British Columbia Court of Appeal is binding on the British Columbia Provincial Court.

Canadian courts also create non-binding decisions. Lower courts do not have to follow rulings made by the courts of other provinces or territories. However, case law from those courts is persuasive. A court may choose whether to apply a non-binding court decision to its case.

Federal Courts

Canada also has the Federal Court and the Federal Court of Appeal. In addition to the SCC, the federal courts have jurisdiction throughout Canada. Federal court justices determine cases of national interest. For example, the federal courts release judgments regarding Indigenous law and national security.

When reviewing the Annotations, you must know the level and the location of the court. With that information, you can accurately assess the degree of influence of the judgment. Finally, knowing how courts have interpreted and applied sections of the Code in the past will help you make an informed decision about how the courts will decide future cases.

EXERCISES

8.7 Subparagraph 1(a)(iii) of section 175 of the Code, Causing Disturbance, Indecent Exhibition, Loitering, Etc., states that everyone who causes a disturbance in or near a public place (not in a dwelling-house) by "impeding or molesting" others has committed the offence. Has it become easier or more difficult to convict on this charge since 1980? (Hint: Look at the Annotations for paragraph 175(1)(a) of the Code.)

_____

_____

_____

_____

_____

8.8 The Quebec case of *R. v. Gouchie* (1976), 33 C.C.C. (2d) 120 (Que. Sess. Peace), referenced in the Annotations for section 343 of the Code, Robbery, was decided by a lower court. Is there another case that might be more persuasive in arguing that a hand gesture does not constitute imitation of an offensive weapon?

_____

_____

_____

_____

_____

Disagreement Among Courts

Provincial and territorial courts may come to different conclusions on the interpretation of a statute. For a binding precedent on a legal issue across Canada, the SCC must make a decision. If the SCC has not made a decision, there is no precedent for lower courts. As a result, contradictory judgments exist among courts at the same level. Therefore, the law is not the same across Canadian provinces and territories.

"*Contra*" preceding a citation indicates that there are contradictory cases in the Annotations. That is, there is a disagreement about a point of law. The decision will be persuasive if the court's analysis of the facts and law relates to your research. However, you must analyze all of the rulings, including decisions that challenge your position.

Example 8.5

Review the Annotations for section 175 of the Code, Causing Disturbance, Indecent Exhibition, Loitering, Etc. under the heading Causing Disturbance (subsec. (1)(a)) / Proof of Disturbance (reproduced below).

There is an example of a disagreement between the Nova Scotia Supreme Court Appeal Division and the Saskatchewan District Court. The contentious issue is the meaning of "swear."

The Nova Scotia Supreme Court Appeal Division in *R. v. Clothier* (1975), 13 N.S.R. (2d) 141 (S.C. App. Div.), held that "swear" should be given its modern meaning of "to use bad or profane or obscene language." In *R. v. Enns* (1968), 5 C.R.N.S. 115, 66 W.W.R. 318 (Sask. Dist. Ct.), the Saskatchewan District Court disagreed and held that swearing is limited to invoking the Deity or something sacred in condemnation of a person or object.

ANNOTATIONS

Causing disturbance (subsec. (1)(*a*)) / Proof of disturbance – Subsection (1)(*a*)(i) requires proof of an externally manifested disturbance of the public peace, in the sense of interference with the ordinary or customary use of the premises by the public. There may be direct evidence of such an effect or interference, or it may be inferred by the evidence of a police officer as to the conduct of a person or persons under subsec. (2). The disturbance may consist of the impugned act itself, as in the case of a fight, interfering with the peaceful use of a barroom, or it may flow as a consequence of the impugned act, as where shouting and swearing produce a scuffle. An interference with the ordinary and customary conduct in or near the public place may consist of something as small as being distracted from one's work, but this interference must be present and must be externally manifested. The disturbance must be one which may reasonably have been foreseen in the particular circumstances of time and place: *R. v. Lohnes*, [1992] 1 S.C.R. 167, 69 C.C.C. (3d) 289.

Proof of disturbance requires that someone was affected or disturbed by the activity. Accordingly, where the accused engaged in a fight in a secluded laneway that was observed by his friends, there was no evidence of anyone being disturbed: *R. v. V.B. (J.G.)* (2002), 165 C.C.C. (3d) 494, 205 N.S.R. (2d) 391 *sub nom. R. v. B. (J.G.V.)* (C.A.).

One may be convicted of an attempt to cause a disturbance: *R. v. Kennedy* (1973), 11 C.C.C. (2d) 263, 21 C.R.N.S. 251 (Ont. C.A.).

"Swear" should be given its modern meaning of "to use bad or profane or obscene language" and is not limited to invoking the Deity or something sacred in condemnation of a person or object: *R. v. Clothier* (1975), 13 N.S.R. (2d) 141 (S.C. App. Div.) *Contra: R. v. Enns* (1968), 5 C.R.N.S. 115, 66 W.W.R. 318 (Sask. Dist. Ct.).

In *R. v. Berry* (1980), 56 C.C.C. (2d) 99 (Ont. C.A.), the court overruled *R. v. Goddard* (1971), 4 C.C.C. (2d) 396, [1971] 3 O.R. 517 (H.C.J.), and held that the offence under subsec. (1)(*a*)(iii) "by impeding" does not require proof of an affray, riot or unlawful assembly. The word "disturbance" is to be given its ordinary dictionary meaning.

It would seem that speaking normally into an electronic megaphone can constitute shouting within the meaning of para. (*a*)(i): *R. v. Reed* (1992), 76 C.C.C. (3d) 204 (B.C.C.A.).

A "public disturbance" requires more than a crowd observing — or even shouting anti-police sentiments at — police officers in the course of arrest. In order to satisfy the *actus reus* of causing a public disturbance by using obscene language, the offending language must *cause* an externally manifested disturbance: *R. v. Swinkels* (2010), 263 C.C.C. (3d) 49 (Ont. C.A.).

EXAMPLE 8.5
CONTRADICTORY
JUDGMENTS

Ratio Decidendi and Obiter Dicta

Ratio decidendi and *obiter dicta* are two statements made by the court. The *ratio decidendi* is the specific ruling or legal principle declared by the court. Readers may refer to the legal principle as the "ratio." It is binding on lower courts.

Obiter dicta (or, in the singular, *obiter dictum*) are legal opinions of the court that do not affect the outcome of the decision. These opinions, referred to as "*obiter*," are generally not binding on lower courts. The exception is *obiter dicta* of the SCC, which are binding on other courts. In *R. v. Sellars*, [1980] 1 S.C.R. 527, the SCC stated that where it rules on a point, any declaration made in the ruling, even though not absolutely necessary to dispose of the appeal, must be followed and applied by all lower courts.

Case Name or Style of Cause

The case name is also the style of cause. In Canada, the case name for criminal cases is generally "*R. v. [the last name of the accused]*." Italics indicate case names in legal texts and law reports.

Why is *R. v. [the last name of the accused]* the citation for a prosecution? *R.* represents either *Regina* (Queen) or *Rex* (King); *v.* is the abbreviation of *versus*, the Latin word meaning "against." Thus, *R. v. Abbott* is read as *Regina* (or *Rex* if the ruling monarch is male) *versus Abbott*.

Canada is a constitutional monarchy. Thus, prosecutors of criminal cases represent the reigning monarch, Queen Elizabeth II. The monarch as prosecutor reflects centuries of criminal law in the United Kingdom of Great Britain and Northern Ireland. Historically, all offences were a breach of the monarch's peace and protection sheltering every citizen of the realm. In contrast, in the republic of the United States of America, the prosecutor represents "The People." For example, a case name from the United States of America is *United States v. Potts*.

Why Does the Case Name Use Initials?

The case name uses initials when the court prevents the publication of the name of the accused. The most common example is a case involving a young person. The *Youth Criminal Justice Act* prohibits the disclosure of the young person's identity.

Additionally, a court order may prohibit the publication of the name of an adult accused. For example, in a sexual offence case, the publication of the name of the accused may reveal the identity of a complainant. As a result, the court will order non-publication of the accused's name and the complainant's name.

An example of a sexual offence case is *R. v. A.(A.)* (2001), 155 C.C.C. (3d) 279 (Ont. C.A.), which is located under the Annotations for section 273.1 of the Code. At the first trial, the judge made an order banning the publication of the name of the complainant but not the name of the accused. The Court of

Appeal ordered a new trial, banned publication of the identity of the complainant, and prohibited publication of the identity of the accused. The publication of the accused's name would likely reveal the identity of the complainant.

A publication prohibition continues until the court orders otherwise. Legislation such as section 486.4 of the Code or section 110 or 111 of the *Youth Criminal Justice Act* permits a judge to create a non-publication order. A judge may also make a non-publication order based on common law powers. If there is a breach of a non-publication order, it is an offence under the relevant statute or by contempt.

Legal Citations

A legal citation includes the case name or style of cause. A citation indicates where to find the full-text judgment. More than one law reporter may report or publish the same case. Thus, there may be multiple reporters for any particular case, often referred to as parallel citations. Therefore, the researcher has choices about where to find the case. However, a legal citation may not include all published reporters. The following is a list of reports:

	ABBREVIATION	TITLE
Canadian reports	Alta. L.R.	Alberta Law Reports
	A.R.	Alberta Reports
	B.C.L.R.	British Columbia Law Reports
	C.C.C.	Canadian Criminal Cases
	C.R.	Criminal Reports
	C.R.N.S.	Criminal Reports New Series
	D.L.R.	Dominion Law Reports
	Man. R.	Manitoba Reports
	M.V.R.	Motor Vehicle Reports
	N.B.R.	New Brunswick Reports
	Nfld. & P.E.I.R.	Newfoundland and Prince Edward Island Reports
	N.R.	National Reporter
	N.S.R.	Nova Scotia Reports
	N.W.T.R	Northwest Territories Reports

(Continued on the next page.)

	ABBREVIATION	TITLE
	O.A.C.	Ontario Appeal Cases
	O.L.R.	Ontario Law Reports
	O.R.	Ontario Reports
	R.J.Q.	Receuils de jurisprudence du Quebec
	Sask. R.	Saskatchewan Reports
	S.C.R.	Supreme Court Reports
	W.A.C.	Western Appeal Cases
	W.C.B.	Weekly Criminal Bulletin
	W.W.R.	Western Weekly Reports
	Y.R.	Yukon Reports
English criminal law reports	Cr. App. R.	Criminal Appeal Reports

Example 8.6

Review *R. v. Harricharan* (1995), 98 C.C.C. (3d) 145, 23 O.R. (3d) 233 (C.A.), in the Annotations for section 436 of the Code, Arson by Negligence (reproduced below).

For this case, there are citations for the *Canadian Criminal Cases* (C.C.C.) and the *Ontario Reports* (O.R.). The number preceding the report name—for example, "23" preceding "O.R."—refers to the volume number of the report. The notation "(3d)" following "O.R." refers to "third series." The number "233" following "(3d)" refers to the number of the page on which the case report begins. In other words, readers can find this case on page 233 of volume 23 of the third series of the *Ontario Reports*.

➲

EXAMPLE 8.6
READING CASE
CITATIONS

ANNOTATIONS
This provision imposes a duty to prevent or control the spread of fires and thus an accused may be convicted under this section even if the fire may have originally been caused by an agency other than that of the accused. The section does, however, require proof of a causal connection between the accused's breach of duty, the resulting spread of the fire, and the injury or damage: *R. v. Harricharan* (1995), 98 C.C.C. (3d) 145, 23 O.R. (3d) 233 (C.A.).

At the end of the citation is "(C.A.)." The initials in the brackets indicate the court level. A court of appeal released this decision. However, which court of appeal? The O.R. only publish decisions from the Province of Ontario. Thus, the court must be the Ontario Court of Appeal.

The year following the case name is the year of publication of the written judgment. The release date of the judgment is not always the same as the year of publication. There may be a delay from the judge providing the decision to the parties and a law report publishing the written judgment.

The year in the above example, 1995, includes round brackets. Round brackets indicate that readers do need to know the year in order to look up the judgment. For both the C.C.C. and the O.R., the volume number alone indicates where they can find the case report.

Example 8.7

Square brackets indicate that the year is required to locate the decision. For example, each volume of the *Supreme Court Reports* (S.C.R.) includes the year printed on the spine. An example is *R. v. Stinchcombe*, the first case cited in the Annotations for section 603 of the Code (reproduced below). The notation "[1991] 3" states that the judgment can be found in the third volume of the reports of cases decided by the SCC in the year 1991.

ANNOTATIONS

Disclosure generally – At least in the case of indictable offences, the Crown is required to produce to the defence all relevant information whether or not the Crown intends to introduce it into evidence and whether it is inculpatory or exculpatory. The Crown does have a discretion to withhold information and as to the timing of the disclosure where necessary to protect the identity of an informer or a continuing investigation. A discretion must also be exercised with respect to the relevance of information. The exercise of this discretion is reviewable by the trial judge who will be guided by the general principle that information ought not to be withheld if there is a reasonable possibility that the withholding of information will impair the right of the accused to make full answer and defence, unless the non-disclosure is justified by the law of privilege. Even then, the trial judge might conclude that the recognition of an existing privilege does not constitute a reasonable limit on the constitutional right to make full answer and defence and thus require disclosure in spite of the law of privilege. Initial disclosure should occur before the accused is called upon to elect the mode of trial or to plead. The obligation to disclose will be triggered by a request by or on behalf of the accused. In the case of an unrepresented accused, the trial judge should not take a plea unless satisfied that the accused has been informed of his right to disclosure: *R. v. Stinchcombe*, [1991] 3 S.C.R. 326, 68 C.C.C. (3d) 1 (7:0).

Production of witness' statement – Subject to the discretion discussed above under the heading "Disclosure generally", the Crown must disclose any statements in its possession of witnesses the Crown proposes to call and all statements obtained from persons who have provided relevant information to the authorities notwithstanding that they are not proposed as Crown witnesses. Where statements are not in existence, other information such as notes should be produced, and, if there are no notes, then in addition to the name, address and occupation of the witness, all information in the possession of the prosecution relating to any relevant evidence that the person could give should be disclosed: *R. v. Stinchcombe, supra*.

Production of accused's statement – The phrase "his own statement" in para. (*a*) includes the accused's statement to the police and not merely the statement given pursuant to s. 541 at the preliminary hearing. Further, even apart from this section, the trial judge has a discretion which, absent some cogent reason, he should exercise to order the Crown to produce the accused's statement for the defence even if the Crown has no intention of introducing the statement as part of its case: *R. v. Savion and Mizrahi* (1980), 52 C.C.C. (2d) 276 (Ont. C.A.). Folld: *R. v. Gonneville* (1982), 69 C.C.C. (2d) 269 (Que. S.C.).

EXAMPLE 8.7
READING CASE
CITATIONS

Infra and Supra

Martin's uses the Latin terms *infra* and *supra*. *Infra* and *supra* may replace the full case citation. *Infra* or *supra* may also indicate where to find additional information in the text about the case. *Infra* indicates that additional information is located later in the text.

Example 8.8

Find the Annotations for section 462.33 of the Code (reproduced below). Review the reference to the case of *Quebec (Attorney General) v. Laroche,* which lists the citation and then states, "see note of this case under s. 462.34, *infra.*"

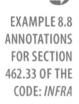

EXAMPLE 8.8 ANNOTATIONS FOR SECTION 462.33 OF THE CODE: *INFRA*

ANNOTATIONS

An order made under this section is a seizure within the meaning of s. 8 of the *Canadian Charter of Rights and Freedoms*. However, the owner's rights under s. 8 were not violated because an agent of a provincial regulatory authority conducting an audit of the owner's business for compliance with provincial statutes passed on to the police information later used in a criminal investigation. The owner was required to keep the information under the provincial legislation and must have known that the legislation was not private in relation to the government. Transmitting information to the police, to initiate an investigation into the irregularities that had been observed, was connected with performance of the agent's duties and that information could be used by the police to support an application for an order under this section: *Quebec (Attorney General) v. Laroche,* [2002] 3 S.C.R. 708, 169 C.C.C. (3d)

Next, find the Annotations for section 462.34 of the Code. Specifically, review the paragraph following the heading Standard of Review (reproduced below). You will find further discussion of *Quebec (Attorney General) v. Laroche* in the commentary for section 462.33 of the Code.

EXAMPLE 8.8 ANNOTATIONS FOR SECTION 462.34 OF THE CODE

ANNOTATIONS

Standard of review – The review of a special warrant or restraint order which is designed to prevent the depletion of illegal property requires a different approach than that used in reviewing wiretap authorizations. The reviewing judge must determine whether the same decision would have been made, not merely whether there was a sufficient basis for the decision. In so doing, the judge must consider any evidence presented by the applicant to rebut or undermine the justifications for the authorization. Even if the judge concludes that the authorization should not have been granted, the Crown may request that the property remain under restraint if it is still required for a criminal investigation or as evidence in other cases. In addition, the rule against collateral attack is also relaxed to accommodate challenges to the underlying general search warrant while reviewing a special warrant or restraint order. *Quebec (Attorney General) v. Laroche,* [2002] 3 S.C.R. 708, 169 C.C.C. (3d) 97.

Supra refers readers to an earlier part of the text. *Supra* appears immediately following a case name and indicates that Martin's has previously cited the case. The editors of the text chose not to repeat the full citation.

Example 8.9

Review the Annotations for section 603 of the Code, Right of Accused, following the heading Disclosure Generally (reproduced below). There is a reference to *R. v. Stinchcombe* with citations. The next paragraph contains another reference to the same case but uses *supra* instead of the citations. *Supra* refers you back to the previous paragraph to find the citations.

ANNOTATIONS

Disclosure generally – At least in the case of indictable offences, the Crown is required to produce to the defence all relevant information whether or not the Crown intends to introduce it into evidence and whether it is inculpatory or exculpatory. The Crown does have a discretion to withhold information and as to the timing of the disclosure where necessary to protect the identity of an informer or a continuing investigation. A discretion must also be exercised with respect to the relevance of information. The exercise of this discretion is reviewable by the trial judge who will be guided by the general principle that information ought not to be withheld if there is a reasonable possibility that the withholding of information will impair the right of the accused to make full answer and defence, unless the non-disclosure is justified by the law of privilege. Even then, the trial judge might conclude that the recognition of an existing privilege does not constitute a reasonable limit on the constitutional right to make full answer and defence and thus require disclosure in spite of the law of privilege. Initial disclosure should occur before the accused is called upon to elect the mode of trial or to plead. The obligation to disclose will be triggered by a request by or on behalf of the accused. In the case of an unrepresented accused, the trial judge should not take a plea unless satisfied that the accused has been informed of his right to disclosure: *R. v. Stinchcombe*, [1991] 3 S.C.R. 326, 68 C.C.C. (3d) 1 (7:0).

Production of witness' statement – Subject to the discretion discussed above under the heading "Disclosure generally", the Crown must disclose any statements in its possession of witnesses the Crown proposes to call and all statements obtained from persons who have provided relevant information to the authorities notwithstanding that they are not proposed as Crown witnesses. Where statements are not in existence, other information such as notes should be produced, and, if there are no notes, then in addition to the name, address and occupation of the witness, all information in the possession of the prosecution relating to any relevant evidence that the person could give should be disclosed: *R. v. Stinchcombe, supra*.

EXAMPLE 8.9
FIRST
REFERENCE

EXAMPLE 8.9
SECOND
REFERENCE:
SUPRA

Impact of the Charter on Judgments

The Charter came into force on April 17, 1982. There were judicial decisions prior to its enactment, so remember to use caution when analyzing the rulings in cases decided prior to that date. Canadian law recognized many of the rights and principles of fundamental justice guaranteed by the Charter before its enactment. Importantly, these rights and principles achieved constitutional status when the Charter was included in the *Constitution Act, 1982*.

The SCC distinguished the Charter from the *Canadian Bill of Rights*, which was the primary statute providing for rights prior to the Charter.

Whereas the *Canadian Bill of Rights* is an act of Parliament, the Charter is a purposive constitutional document. First, the courts have more discretion in their interpretation of the rights asserted by the Charter. Second, the courts have interpreted those rights in a broader fashion. As a result, judgments in the Charter era have made significant changes to Canadian law.

When reading the Annotations, be aware of the date of the judicial decision. Did the court make the decision prior to 1982? If so, the court rulings may not be "good law."

After 1982, the courts re-examined legal issues in light of the Charter. Thus, the court decision and reasoning from earlier decisions are no longer legally correct in Canada. In other words, the law has changed. Martin's includes information about changes due to the Charter in the Annotations.

There have been more than 35 years of legal decisions since the enactment of the Charter. However, the courts continue to examine issues within its context. Lower courts have made Charter rulings, but we are still waiting for further Charter rulings from the SCC. As a result, there is still uncertainty about the impact of the Charter on criminal law and criminal procedure.

Example 8.10

Review the Annotations for section 5 of the *Canada Evidence Act* following the heading Effect of S.13 of the Charter of Rights [subsec. (2)] (reproduced below). There is a reference to the judgment of the SCC in *R. v. Nedelcu*, [2012] 2 S.C.R. 311. The SCC decided that the court at criminal trials could allow the Crown to cross-examine the accused on the non-incriminatory parts of his civil discovery transcript to impeach the accused's testimony. Furthermore, Martin's states that readers must review cases decided prior to *R. v. Nedelcu* carefully because the decision is narrow in scope.

Effect of s. 13 of the Charter of Rights [subsec. (2)] – Cases under this subsection must now be considered in light of s. 13 of the *Canadian Charter of Rights and Freedoms*. Cases decided prior to *R. v. Nedelcu*, [2012] 3 S.C.R. 311, 290 C.C.C. (3d) 153, must be read in light of its relatively narrow holding discussed below. In *R. v. Dubois*, [1985] 2 S.C.R. 350, 22 C.C.C. (3d) 513 (6:1), the court held that: (1) section 13 applies although the first proceeding took place prior to the Charter's proclamation; (2) section 13 applies to a technically voluntary witness such as the accused at his own trial and its protection does not depend on an objection, unlike this subsection; (3) the evidence need not have been incriminating in the first proceedings; (4) the retrial of the same offence following an appeal is another proceeding and the accused's testimony at the first trial can therefore not be tendered at the second trial as part of the Crown's case.

In *R. v. Henry*, [2005] 3 S.C.R. 609, 202 C.C.C. (3d) 449, the court overruled its earlier decision in *R. v. Mannion*, [1986] 2 S.C.R. 272, 28 C.C.C. (3d) 544, and held that s. 13 is not available to an accused who chooses to testify at his or her retrial on the same indictment.

In *R. v. Nedelcu*, *supra*, the court (6:3) held that the Crown was entitled to cross-examine the accused on the *non-incriminatory* portions of his civil discovery transcript for impeachment purposes at his criminal trial. Incriminating evidence is evidence given by the witness at the prior proceeding that the Crown could use at the subsequent proceeding, if it were permitted to do so, to prove guilt, *i.e.*, to prove or assist in proving one or more of the essential elements of the offence for which the witness is being tried. Where the evidence given by the witness at the prior proceeding could not be used by the Crown at the subsequent proceeding to prove the witness's guilt on the charge for which he or she is being tried, the prior evidence is not "incriminating evidence" and can be used to test the accused's credibility.

Section 13 of the Charter is violated by testimony of a police officer that he was able to identify the accused as a result of hearing him testify in another proceeding: *R. v. Skinner* (1988), 42 C.C.C. (3d) 575 (Ont. C.A.).

A witness's knowledge of immunity from the use of testimony to incriminate them is rarely relevant to credibility. Inquiries into a witness's knowledge of this provision may deflect the jury's attention away from the real issues and may impinge upon confidential solicitor-client communications. Without further evidence of a motive for falsely testifying, a witness's knowledge of s. 13 standing alone does not constitute a motive to lie and cannot affect the witness's credibility: *R. v. Jabarianha*, [2001] 3 S.C.R. 430, 159 C.C.C. (3d) 1.

In *R. v. Jabarianha*, *supra*, the court approved *R. v. Swick* (1997), 118 C.C.C. (3d) 33, 150 D.L.R. (4th) 566 (Ont. C.A.), and held that the probative value of a witness's knowledge of s. 13 of the Charter will generally be overborne by its prejudicial effect. Crown counsel should rarely be permitted to cross-examine on a witness's knowledge of s. 13. A witness's knowledge of the law is not co-extensive with a tendency to lie. Without other evidence of a motive for testifying falsely, evidence of a witness's knowledge of s. 13 of the Charter should not affect his or her credibility. In rare circumstances, cross-examination of a witness's knowledge of s. 13 may be permitted. If the Crown provided some evidence of a plot to lie or to obtain favours, the probative value of a witness's knowledge of s. 13 could outweigh its prejudicial effect whereas evidence of mere friendship between the accused and witness will not. Similarly, *R. v. Noël*, [2002] 3 S.C.R. 433, 168 C.C.C. (3d) 193.

C

EXAMPLE 8.10
EFFECT OF THE
CHARTER

CHAPTER 9

Shaded Text

Introduction

Martin's Annual Criminal Code uses shaded text to indicate to the reader that the text is an addition to the text by the editor and not part of the statute. Generally, shaded text identifies an amendment of the statute that is *not yet in force* or a *regulation*. It may also be an editor's note.

Amendments

A shaded box displays amendments not yet in force at the date of the printing of Martin's. Thus, the reader must research whether the amendment is currently in force. To determine the current wording of a statute, the reader must review the Department of Justice website at <https://laws.justice.gc.ca/eng>.

Example 9.1

In the 2020 edition of Martin's, there is a note in a shaded box for section 279.01 of the *Criminal Code* (reproduced below) that indicates amendments to the Code. The amendments were not in force at the printing of the 2020 edition. If there is no shading in subsequent editions, these sections have come into force. If the shading remains, the reader must consult the Department of Justice website.

Regulations

Regulations are rules made by government administrators under the authority of a statute. Regulations change more often than statutes because regulations do not require the legislative process. They provide details to administer and enforce a statute. As long as they do not contradict a statute, regulations have the force of law.

EXAMPLE 9.1
AMENDMENTS
THAT ARE NOT
YET IN FORCE

Note: Section 279.01 amended by enacting subsec. (3), 2015, c. 16, s. 1 (to come into force by order of the Governor in Council):

Presumption

(3) For the purposes of subsections (1) and 279.011(1), evidence that a person who is not exploited lives with or is habitually in the company of a person who is exploited is, in the absence of evidence to the contrary, proof that the person exercises control, direction or influence over the movements of that person for the purpose of exploiting them or facilitating their exploitation.

Martin's includes regulations made under the authority of the *Firearms Act*. The regulations assist in the interpretation of subsection 84(1) and section 117.07 of the Code. Martin's provides the regulations after the commentary for each section. Shading separates the regulations from the rest of the text.

Example 9.2

Following section 117.07 of the Code, Public Officers, are the *Firearms Act Regulations Prescribing Public Officers* (reproduced below). Section 2 of the Regulations states that they came into force on December 1, 1998.

EXAMPLE 9.2
REGULATIONS
UNDER THE
FIREARMS ACT

REGULATIONS PRESCRIBING PUBLIC OFFICERS

1. (1) A member of any of the following classes of persons, if employed in the public service of Canada or by the government of a province or municipality, is a public officer for the purposes of paragraph 117.07(2)(*g*) of the *Criminal Code*:

   (*a*) employees who are responsible for the examination, inventory, storage, maintenance or transportation of court exhibits and evidence;

   (*b*) employees of police forces or other public service agencies who are responsible for the acquisition, examination, inventory, storage, maintenance, issuance or transportation of firearms, prohibited weapons, restricted weapons, prohibited devices, prohibited ammunition or explosive substances;

   (*c*) technicians, laboratory analysts and scientists who work at forensic or research laboratories;

   (*d*) armourers and firearms instructors who work at police academies or similar institutions designated under subparagraph 117.07(2)(*e*)(ii) of the *Criminal Code*, or are employed by a federal or provincial department of natural resources, fisheries, wildlife, conservation or the environment, or by Revenue Canada;

   (*e*) park wardens and other employees of a federal or provincial department who are responsible for the enforcement of laws and regulations dealing with natural resources, fisheries, wildlife, conservation or the environment;

   (*f*) immigration officers;

   (*g*) security personnel employed by the House of Commons or the Senate or by the Service, as defined in section 79.51 of the *Parliament of Canada Act*; and

   (*h*) aircraft pilots employed by the Department of Transport or other public service agencies.

(2) For the purposes of subsection (1), the expression "public service agencies" has the same meaning as in section 1 of the Public Agents Firearms Regulations.

Coming into Force

2. These Regulations come into force on December 1, 1998. **SOR/98-466; SOR/98-472; SOR/2011-68; SOR/2015-166, s. 1.**

Editor's Note

The authors and editors of Martin's provide additional information about a subject raised in the text. A shaded box beginning with "Editor's Note:" presents the additional explanation.

Example 9.3

There is an editor's note on the second page of the *Controlled Drugs and Substances Act* (reproduced below). The note explains the content, structure, and historical context of the legislation. The Canadian Parliament enacted the Act in 1996 as a replacement for previous statutes addressing the regulation of drugs and narcotics.

Editor's Note: The *Controlled Drugs and Substances Act* creates a new scheme for the regulation of certain dangerous drugs and narcotics, now known as "controlled substances". The Act replaces the *Narcotic Control Act*, R.S.C. 1985, c. N-1 and Part III [Controlled Drugs] and Part IV [Restricted Drugs] of the *Food and Drugs Act*, R.S.C. 1985, c. F-27. The essential scheme of the legislation is similar to the former *Narcotic Control Act* and the *Food and Drugs Act*.

EXAMPLE 9.3
EDITOR'S
EXPLANATION OF
THE CONTENT,
STRUCTURE, AND
HISTORICAL
CONTEXT OF THE
STATUTE

CHAPTER 10

Forms

Introduction

Part XXVIII / Miscellaneous of the *Criminal Code* is the final part of the Code. Criminal proceedings require a general structure for forms. However, subsection 849(1) of the Code states that forms may be "varied to suit the case, or forms to the like effect are deemed to be good, valid and sufficient." Thus, the Code creates flexibility in the structure of the forms. Nevertheless, the forms most often used are those provided in Part XXVIII.

The *Youth Criminal Justice Act* (YCJA, reproduced in *Martin's Annual Criminal Code*) came into force in April 2003. It replaced the *Young Offenders Act*, R.S.C. 1985, c. Y-1. According to section 155 of the YCJA, the governor in council may prescribe forms for proceedings under the Act. In addition, YCJA proceedings may use the forms established by Part XXVIII of the Code. Specifically, subsection 154(2) of the Act is the authority to use Code forms for youth proceedings.

Application of Forms

Review a form authorized under Part XXVIII of the Code. In round brackets, below the form number, there is a reference to the relevant section or subsection.

Example 10.1

Review Form 34.2 (reproduced below). The line below the form number refers to subsection 722(4) of the Code. For information about how to use this form, read section 722 of the Code.

EXAMPLE 10.1
FORM APPLIES
TO THIS
SUBSECTION

FORM 34.2

(Subsection 722(4))

VICTIM IMPACT STATEMENT

This form may be used to provide a description of the physical or emotional harm, property damage or economic loss suffered by you as the result of the commission of an offence, as well as a description of the impact of the offence on you. You may attach additional pages if you need more space.

Your statement must not include

- any statement about the offence or the offender that is not relevant to the harm or loss you suffered;

- any unproven allegations;

- any comments about any offence for which the offender was not convicted;

- any complaint about any individual, other than the offender, who was involved in the investigation or prosecution of the offence; or

- except with the court's approval, an opinion or recommendation about the sentence.

You may present a detailed account of the impact the offence has had on your life. The following sections are examples of information you may wish to include in your statement. You are not required to include all of this information.

Emotional impact

Describe how the offence has affected you emotionally. For example, think of

- your lifestyle and activities;

- your relationships with others such as your spouse, family and friends;

- your ability to work, attend school or study; and

- your feelings, emotions and reactions as they relate to the offence.

_____

_____

_____

_____

Physical impact

Describe how the offence has affected you physically. For example, think of

- ongoing physical pain, discomfort, illness, scarring, disfigurement or physical limitation;

- hospitalization or surgery you have had because of the offence;

- treatment, physiotherapy or medication you have been prescribed;

- the need for any further treatment or the expectation that you will receive further treatment; and

- any permanent or long-term disability.

_____

_____

_____

_____

Economic impact

Describe how the offence has affected you financially. For example, think of

- the value of any property that was lost or damaged and the cost of repairs or replacement;

- any financial loss due to missed time from work;

- the cost of any medical expenses, therapy or counselling;

- any costs or losses that are not covered by insurance.

Please note that this is not an application for compensation or restitution.

_____
_____
_____
_____

Fears for security

Describe any fears you have for your security or that of your family and friends. For example, think of

• concerns with respect to contact with the offender; and

• concerns with respect to contact between the offender and members of your family or close friends.

_____
_____
_____
_____

Drawing, poem or letter

You may use this space to draw a picture or write a poem or letter if it will help you express the impact that the offence has had on you.

I would like to present my statement in court.

To the best of my knowledge, the information contained in this statement is true.

Dated this .... day of .... 20.........., at.......... .

Signature of declarant

If you completed this statement on behalf of the victim, please indicate the reasons why you did so and the nature of your relationship with the victim.

_____
_____

Dated this .... day of .... 20.........., at.......... .

Signature of declarant

2015, c. 13, s. 35.

Under subsection 722(1) of the Code, a "court shall consider any statement of a victim prepared in accordance with this section and filed with the court describing the physical or emotional harm, property damage or economic loss suffered by the victim as the result of the commission of the offence and the impact of the offence on the victim." Finally, according to subsection 722(4) of the Code, the "statement must be prepared in writing, using Form 34.2 in Part XXVIII" of the Code.

EXAMPLE 10.1
FORM APPLIES
TO THIS
SUBSECTION

VICTIM IMPACT STATEMENT / Inquiry by court / Adjournment / Form / Presentation of statement / Photograph / Conditions of exclusion / Consideration of statement / Evidence concerning victim admissible.

722. (1) When determining the sentence to be imposed on an offender or determining whether the offender should be discharged under section 730 in respect of any offence, the court shall consider any statement of a victim prepared in accordance with this section and filed with the court describing the physical or emotional harm, property damage or economic loss suffered by the victim as the result of the commission of the offence and the impact of the offence on the victim.

(2) As soon as feasible after a finding of guilt and in any event before imposing sentence, the court shall inquire of the prosecutor if reasonable steps have been taken to provide the victim with an opportunity to prepare a statement referred to in subsection (1).

(3) On application of the prosecutor or a victim or on its own motion, the court may adjourn the proceedings to permit the victim to prepare a statement referred to in subsection (1) or to present evidence in accordance with subsection (9), if the court is satisfied that the adjournment would not interfere with the proper administration of justice.

(4) The statement must be prepared in writing, using Form 34.2 in Part XXVIII, in accordance with the procedures established by a program designated for that purpose by the lieutenant governor in council of the province in which the court is exercising its jurisdiction.

(5) The court shall, on the request of a victim, permit the victim to present the statement by

    (*a*) reading it;
    (*b*) reading it in the presence and close proximity of any support person of the victim's choice;
    (*c*) reading it outside the court room or behind a screen or other device that would allow the victim not to see the offender; or
    (*d*) presenting it in any other manner that the court considers appropriate.

(6) During the presentation
    (*a*) the victim may have with them a photograph of themselves taken before the commission of the offence if it would not, in the opinion of the court, disrupt the proceedings; or
    (*b*) if the statement is presented by someone acting on the victim's behalf, that individual may have with them a photograph of the victim taken before the commission of the offence if it would not, in the opinion of the court, disrupt the proceedings.

(7) The victim shall not present the statement outside the court room unless arrangements are made for the offender and the judge or justice to watch the presentation by means of closed-circuit television or otherwise and the offender is permitted to communicate with counsel while watching the presentation.

(8) In considering the statement, the court shall take into account the portions of the statement that it considers relevant to the determination referred to in subsection (1) and disregard any other portion.

(9) Whether or not a statement has been prepared and filed in accordance with this section, the court may consider any other evidence concerning any victim of the offence for the purpose of determining the sentence to be imposed on the offender or whether the offender should be discharged under section 730. 1995, c. 22, s. 6; 1999, c. 25, s. 17; 2000, c. 12, s. 95(*d*); 2015, c. 13, s. 25.

Lastly, the referenced section or subsection provides additional information to the reader about the form.

10.1   Review Form 7.1, Warrant to Enter Dwelling-House. Where will the reader find more information about the form?

_____

_____

_____

_____

_____

10.2   Review Form 6, Summons to a Person Charged with an Offence. Where will the reader find more information about the form?

_____

_____

_____

_____

10.3   Review Form 2, Information. What is the purpose of this form?

_____

_____

_____

_____

_____

CHAPTER 11

Appendix / Forms of Charges

Introduction

The final portion of *Martin's Annual Criminal Code* is the Appendix / Forms of Charges. This section includes the suggested wording for charges under the *Criminal Code* and the *Controlled Drugs and Substances Act* (CDSA). The common offences that accused are charged with are included in the Appendix / Forms of Charges. For other offences, and in cases with complex fact patterns, law enforcement professionals must consult the Crown attorney's office.

Information (Form 2)

Law enforcement professionals charge accused with offences. As a result, an accused must know the offence that law enforcement professionals believe he or she has committed. How do law enforcement professionals notify the accused about the offence? In Canada, an Information is the primary charging document. The form used for an Information is Form 2 (reproduced on the next page), which is located in Part XXVIII / Miscellaneous of the Code.

The Information starts all criminal prosecutions. The court requires specific charge wording for an Information (Form 2). Any error in the wording of a charge may result in delay of the prosecution. Furthermore, the court may declare a charge a nullity. Specifically, the court may order the prosecution of a criminal charge to cease. Thus, knowing how to use the accepted charge wording is crucial for law enforcement professionals.

The Appendix / Forms of Charges provides the suggested charge wording for each offence in the Code and the CDSA. First, the reader will consult the specific criminal offence in the Appendix / Forms of Charges. Second, "The informant says that" is the wording that starts a charge. Third, immediately following "The Informant says that," the writer adds the charge wording to complete the Information (Form 2).

WHERE THE
CHARGE
WORDING IS
INSERTED

FORM 2

(Sections 506 and 788)

Information

Canada,

Province of ....,

(territorial division).

This is the information of C.D., of ...., *(occupation)*, hereinafter called the informant.

The informant says that (*if the informant has no personal knowledge state that he believes on reasonable grounds and state the offence.*)

Sworn before me this .... day of   ....

........................, A.D. ....,   *(Signature of Informant)*

at ....

....

A Justice of the Peace in and

for ....

Note: The date of birth of the accused may be mentioned on the information or indictment.

Correctly Completing the Information (Form 2)

Criminal law and criminal procedure developed from English common law, including principles designed to protect the individual from arbitrary treatment by the state. In Canada, both the Code and the *Canadian Charter of Rights and Freedoms* include criminal law and criminal procedure. Furthermore, Canadian social and political thinking emphasizes personal liberty. Thus, the courts strictly interpret laws that impose criminal sanctions upon a person. Additionally, criminal law and criminal procedure must be known and accessible to the public, clearly defined, and consistently applied.

If the state alleges that a person has committed a criminal offence, the charge must comply with criminal law and criminal procedure. Canadian criminal law and criminal procedure ensure that the charging documents disclose data to the accused person to identify the criminal course of conduct or criminal transaction. Furthermore, the charge must specify all of the elements of the offence alleged to have been committed. Finally, an Information must ensure that the accused is able to provide a full answer and a defence to the accusation.

Elements of the Offence and Sentencing

The Code addresses two aspects of each offence: the elements of the offence and available sentences. The elements of the offence are the criteria that define the offence. Every criminal offence provides available sentences for the court to consider. The sentence provision states that a person "is guilty of an offence," the type of offence, and the maximum sentence available for that offence. If the offence is a summary conviction offence, the maximum sentence is two years less a day in custody and a $5,000 fine according to subsection 787(1) of the Code. Thus, a summary conviction offence will not state the maximum sentence.

Example 11.1

Review section 175 of the Code, Causing Disturbance, Indecent Exhibition, Loitering, Etc. (reproduced below).

Subsection 175(1) of the Code describes the elements of the offence of causing disturbance. It also includes the available sentences at the end of the subsection. Specifically, subsection 175(1) of the Code states, "Every one who … is guilty of an offence punishable on summary conviction."

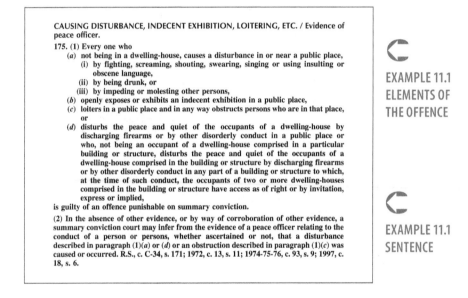

CAUSING DISTURBANCE, INDECENT EXHIBITION, LOITERING, ETC. / Evidence of peace officer.

175. (1) Every one who
   (*a*) not being in a dwelling-house, causes a disturbance in or near a public place,
      (i) by fighting, screaming, shouting, swearing, singing or using insulting or obscene language,
      (ii) by being drunk, or
      (iii) by impeding or molesting other persons,
   (*b*) openly exposes or exhibits an indecent exhibition in a public place,
   (*c*) loiters in a public place and in any way obstructs persons who are in that place, or
   (*d*) disturbs the peace and quiet of the occupants of a dwelling-house by discharging firearms or by other disorderly conduct in a public place or who, not being an occupant of a dwelling-house comprised in a particular building or structure, disturbs the peace and quiet of the occupants of a dwelling-house comprised in the building or structure by discharging firearms or by other disorderly conduct in any part of a building or structure to which, at the time of such conduct, the occupants of two or more dwelling-houses comprised in the building or structure have access as of right or by invitation, express or implied,
is guilty of an offence punishable on summary conviction.

(2) In the absence of other evidence, or by way of corroboration of other evidence, a summary conviction court may infer from the evidence of a peace officer relating to the conduct of a person or persons, whether ascertained or not, that a disturbance described in paragraph (1)(*a*) or (*d*) or an obstruction described in paragraph (1)(*c*) was caused or occurred. R.S., c. C-34, s. 171; 1972, c. 13, s. 11; 1974-75-76, c. 93, s. 9; 1997, c. 18, s. 6.

EXAMPLE 11.1 ELEMENTS OF THE OFFENCE

EXAMPLE 11.1 SENTENCE

In Example 11.1, subsection 175(1) of the Code describes the elements of the offence and ends with sentence options. However, the available sentences may be in a separate section of the statute.

Example 11.2

Review section 265 of the Code, Assault (reproduced below).

Section 265 describes the elements of the offence of assault. However, the section does not discuss the sentence options. The Cross-References for section 265 state that section 266 of the Code is the "punishment for assault simpliciter [formerly common assault]" (reproduced below).

**EXAMPLE 11.2
ELEMENTS OF
THE OFFENCE**

ASSAULT / Application / Consent / Accused's belief as to consent.

265. (1) A person commits an assault when
   (a) without the consent of another person, he applies force intentionally to that other person, directly or indirectly;
   (b) he attempts or threatens, by an act or a gesture, to apply force to another person, if he has, or causes that other person to believe upon reasonable grounds that he has, present ability to effect his purpose; or
   (c) while openly wearing or carrying a weapon or an imitation thereof, he accosts or impedes another person or begs.

(2) This section applies to all forms of assault, including sexual assault, sexual assault with a weapon, threats to a third party or causing bodily harm and aggravated sexual assault.

(3) For the purposes of this section, no consent is obtained where the complainant submits or does not resist by reason of
   (a) the application of force to the complainant or to a person other than the complainant;
   (b) threats or fear of the application of force to the complainant or to a person other than the complainant;
   (c) fraud; or
   (d) the exercise of authority.

(4) Where an accused alleges that he believed that the complainant consented to the conduct that is the subject-matter of the charge, a judge, if satisfied that there is sufficient evidence and that, if believed by the jury, the evidence would constitute a defence, shall instruct the jury, when reviewing all the evidence relating to the determination of the honesty of the accused's belief, to consider the presence or absence of reasonable grounds for that belief. R.S., c. C-34, s. 244; 1974-75-76, c. 93, s. 21; 1980-81-82-83, c. 125, s. 19.

CROSS-REFERENCES

The terms "complainant" and "weapon" are defined in s. 2. The offences described in subsec. (2) may be found as follows: s. 266, punishment for assault *simpliciter* [formerly common assault]; s. 267, assault with weapon and assault causing bodily harm; s. 268, aggravated assault; s. 270, assault police; s. 271, sexual assault; s. 272, sexual assault with weapon, threats to a third party and causing bodily harm; s. 273, aggravated sexual assault.

As to defences see: s. 16, insanity; s. 17, compulsion by threats; s. 25, use of force in enforcement of law; s. 27, use of force to prevent commission of certain offences; s. 33.1 intoxication; ss. 34 to 37, self defence and defence of person under accused's protection; ss. 38 to 41, defence of property; s. 43, use of force by way of correction; s. 44, use of force by master of vessel.

As to notes respecting the intoxication and necessity defences see s. 8. These latter defences, especially intoxication are of limited application since most of the assault offences are general intent offences.

Section 273.1 defines consent for the sexual offences in ss. 271, 272 and 273 and, in particular, defines circumstances additional to those set out in s. 265(3) in which no consent is obtained. For the same group of offences, s. 273.2 sets out circumstances where belief in consent is not a defence. For additional notes concerning the defence of honest belief in consent, see the notes following s. 273.2.

As to mode of trial and punishment, see the cross-references under particular assault offence.

**EXAMPLE 11.2
WHERE TO FIND
AVAILABLE
SENTENCES**

ASSAULT.

266. Every one who commits an assault is guilty of
   (a) an indictable offence and liable to imprisonment for a term not exceeding five years; or
   (b) an offence punishable on summary conviction. R.S., c. C-34, s. 245; 1972, c. 13, s. 21; 1974-75-76, c. 93, s. 22; 1980-81-82-83, c. 125, s. 19.

To properly complete an Information (Form 2), you must correctly identify the sentence provision. The sentence provision must be inserted into the Information. Specifically, the charge wording ends with "contrary *etc.*" You will replace "*etc.*" with the sentence provision. For example, review section 268 of the Code in the Appendix / Forms of Charges. You will replace "thereby committing an aggravated assault contrary *etc.*" with "thereby committing an aggravated assault contrary to section 268 of the *Criminal Code.*"

It is an error to insert the elements of the offence provision. As a result, where the elements of the offence are in a separate provision from the sentence provision, remember to use the correct provision. If you require assistance finding the sentence provision for a criminal offence, review the Cross-References, the Index, or the Offence Grid.

Requirements for an Information (Form 2)

Drafting (Section 581 of the Code)

Section 581 of the Code, Substance of Offence, governs the drafting of criminal offence charges. The rules ensure that the accused knows the offence and is able to provide a full answer and a defence to the charges.

Review the Synopsis for section 581 of the Code. An Information generally addresses a "single transaction." However, a single transaction may involve a series of events or several complainants. For further clarification of the single transaction rule, review the court decisions included in the Annotations for this section.

According to subsection 581(2) of the Code, there are three permissible methods of stating the offence. The person drafting the Information may use popular language, words from the statute that describes the offence, or language that provides the accused notice of the offence. Nevertheless, most charges are drafted using the words of the section that describes the offence.

Subsection 581(3) of the Code requires that the Information contain details to allow the accused to identify the events leading to the charge. Specifically, the Information must include the date, the place, and the alleged acts or omissions.

Drafting an Information

The most common way to draft an Information (Form 2) is using the wording suggested in the Appendix / Forms of Charges. Find the Appendix / Forms of Charges at the back of Martin's. The suggested wording is organized by section number. Locate the section number for the offence that the accused has allegedly committed.

Before drafting an Information, you should locate the section in the appropriate statute, the Code, or the CDSA. Read the section to ensure that the essential elements required for the criminal offence are included in the wording of the charge. The substantive section outlines the elements of the offence. Remember, however, that the section number for the sentence provision is inserted at the end of the charge, after "contrary *etc.*"

The following examples illustrate how to complete the Information (Form 2) with correct wording for the charge.

Example 11.3

Review the first page in the Appendix / Forms of Charges. The first entry is the offence of "Forging a passport" created by paragraph 57(1)(a) of the Code (reproduced below). The wording in italics contained within square brackets, for example, "[*specify the forged passport*]," is a drafting instruction. It is not part of the wording of the charge. At the end of the charge, "*etc.*" is another drafting instruction and will be replaced by a reference to the sentence provision.

EXAMPLE 11.3
SUGGESTED
WORDING FOR
THE CHARGE

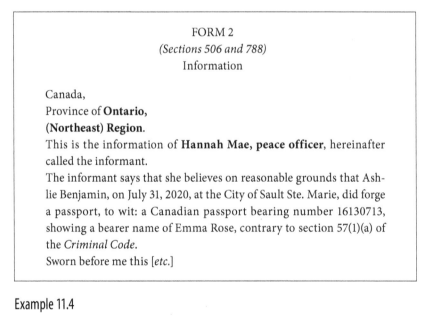

> **FORMS OF CHARGES UNDER THE *CRIMINAL CODE***
>
> **57(1)(*a*) Forging a passport**
>   A.B. on .... at .... did forge a passport [*specify the forged passport*] contrary *etc.*

Insert the wording for the charge into an Information (Form 2) with the details of the allegation. It should look like the following:

> FORM 2
> *(Sections 506 and 788)*
> Information
>
> Canada,
> Province of **Ontario,**
> **(Northeast) Region.**
> This is the information of **Hannah Mae, peace officer**, hereinafter called the informant.
> The informant says that she believes on reasonable grounds that Ashlie Benjamin, on July 31, 2020, at the City of Sault Ste. Marie, did forge a passport, to wit: a Canadian passport bearing number 16130713, showing a bearer name of Emma Rose, contrary to section 57(1)(a) of the *Criminal Code*.
> Sworn before me this [*etc.*]

Example 11.4

Review the second offence listed in the Appendix / Forms of Charges, created by paragraph 57(1)(b) of the Code, "Uttering a forged passport" (reproduced below).

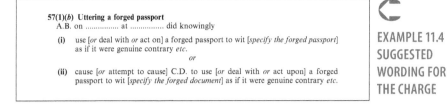

57(1)(*b*) Uttering a forged passport
A.B. on .... at .... did knowingly

(i)   use [*or* deal with *or* act on] a forged passport to wit [*specify the forged passport*] as if it were genuine contrary *etc.*

or

(ii) cause [*or* attempt to cause] C.D. to use [*or* deal with *or* act upon] a forged passport to wit [*specify the forged document*] as if it were genuine contrary *etc.*

EXAMPLE 11.4
SUGGESTED
WORDING FOR
THE CHARGE

The wording in the first set of square brackets has both italics and normal type. The italicized "*or*" is instructional. The normal type is part of the substantive offence. Consequently, the substantive charge for using the forged passport would read as follows:

> Ashlie Benjamin, on July 31, 2020, at the City of Sault Ste. Marie, did knowingly use a forged passport, to wit: a Canadian passport bearing number 16130713, showing a bearer name of Emma Rose, as if it were genuine contrary to section 57(1)(b)(i) of the *Criminal Code*.

Alternatively, the charge may state "did knowingly deal with … *etc.*" Furthermore, that charge may state "did knowingly act on … *etc.*" All of the suggested charge wordings under subparagraph 57(1)(b)(i) of the Code are ways that an accused person may commit the criminal offence. Most Crown attorneys want the Information (Form 2) completed in the broadest way permissible by law. Because the offence created by subparagraph 57(1)(b)(i) of the Code may be committed in any manner stated, that is, using, dealing with, or acting on the forged passport, the information may be worded as follows:

> Ashlie Benjamin, on July 31, 2020, at the City of Sault Ste. Marie, did knowingly use, deal with or act on a forged passport, to wit: a Canadian passport bearing number 16130713, showing a bearer name of Emma Rose, contrary to section 57(1)(b)(i) of the *Criminal Code*.

The italicized "*or*" is instructional. However, it may be included in the body of the charge. Offences that can be committed in alternative ways should be charged in the broadest terms possible.

Multiple Accused

The Appendix / Forms of Charges provides the wording for a singular accused person. However, two or more individuals may be charged on the same Information. Specifically, the charge will start with "A.B. and C.D. did commit the criminal offence." Nevertheless, the substantive wording of the draft charges in the Appendix / Forms of Charges remains the same.

Example 11.5

Review page A/63 in the Appendix / Forms of Charges. The first entry is the offence of "Conspiracy to murder," created by paragraph 465(1)(a) of the Code (reproduced below). The wording of the charge starts with "A.B. and C.D. on ... at ... did conspire together to murder ... ." The initials "A.B." and "C.D." will be replaced by the names of the persons accused with conspiracy. Finally, more than two persons may be accused of the same criminal offence.

EXAMPLE 11.5 SUGGESTED WORDING FOR MULTIPLE ACCUSED

> **465(1)(a) Conspiracy to murder**
>   A.B. and C.D. on .... at .... did conspire together to murder E.F. [*or to* cause E.F. to be murdered] contrary *etc.*

Multiple Charges

The Information may charge an accused with more than one offence. In this case, each separate charge is set out as a separate "count." Each count is numbered. For example, A.B. is alleged to have committed theft and mischief. Count 1 sets out the charge of theft, for example, "Count 1: A.B. on ... at ... did steal ... " followed by the words "and further that," followed by "Count 2: A.B. did commit mischief by ... ."

Details Missing (Section 583 of the Code)

It is permissible for details to be missing from the charge. More particularly, according to section 583 of the Code, Certain Omissions not Grounds for Objection, missing details may include the complainant's name, a precise description of the place, and how the accused committed the alleged offence. However, the absence of these details must not prevent the accused from exercising the right to a full answer and a defence to the charge. Furthermore, the absence of these details must not prevent a fair trial.

Particulars (Section 587 of the Code)

Particulars are details that an accused requires to make a full answer and a defence. Particulars also ensure a fair trial for the accused. Under section 587 of the Code, if an accused person requires data that the prosecutor has not provided, the accused applies to the court for particulars about the alleged crime. If the court agrees with the accused, a court will order the prosecutor to provide additional data to the accused.

11.1 The law enforcement professional gathered the following facts. Cynthia Davidson had her Mighty lawn mower (model number 13-E) stolen from her home in the city of Kenora by the accused, André Boucher, on July 15, 2020. Ms Davidson recently purchased the lawn mower for approximately $400. Under what section would Mr. Boucher be charged?

_____

_____

_____

_____

_____

11.2 What might the charge state?

_____

_____

_____

_____

11.3 Compare this charge with the requirements set out in section 581 of the Code. Does it provide Mr. Boucher with sufficient data to be able to identify the transaction and the offence?

_____

_____

_____

_____

_____

11.4 Where can you find all of the elements of the offence of theft required before Mr. Boucher can be charged?

_____

_____

_____

_____

_____

11.5 The charge does not include any data about how Mr. Boucher obtained Ms Davidson's lawn mower. Is this a problem?

_____

_____

_____

_____

_____

11.6 How can Mr. Boucher request additional data about how he was alleged to have committed the offence?

_____

_____

_____

_____

_____

11.7 There is a complaint from Caroline Dennhardt that her ex-boyfriend, Andrew Bennett, repeatedly communicated with her, against her wishes, between July 31, 2020 and August 29, 2020 in the city of Ottawa. Mr. Bennett sent flowers and cards. He also texted her requesting reconciliation. At Ms Dennhardt's request, a law enforcement professional asked Mr. Bennett to stop. Nevertheless, Mr. Bennett continued the behaviour. If the allegations can be proved, where in the Code will you find the elements of the offence?

_____

_____

_____

_____

_____

11.8 Look at the suggested wording (in the Appendix / Forms of Charges) immediately following paragraph 264(2)(d) of the Code: "thereby caus-ing C.D. to reasonably, in all the circumstances, fear for her safety … contrary _etc._" Does this relate only to "engaging in threatening con-duct," as prohibited by paragraph 264(2)(d) of the Code, or does it re-late to one or more of the other paragraphs, such as paragraph 264(2)(b) of the Code?

_____

_____

_____

_____

_____

11.9 How should the charge against Mr. Bennett be completed?

_____

_____

_____

_____

_____

11.10   Why is subsection 264(3) of the Code used instead of paragraph 264(2)(b) of the Code?

_____

_____

_____

_____

_____

CHAPTER 12

Conclusion

Martin's Annual Criminal Code contains a wealth of information, and it includes research tools to improve your analysis of legal questions. When you research criminal law issues, Martin's is an excellent place to start!

After reading this guide, reviewing the examples, and completing the exercises, you should be able to navigate Martin's. Finally, by learning how to navigate Martin's, you now have the skills to navigate other annotated texts.